THE HEALING POWER OF
LOVING-KINDNESS

Also by Tulku Thondup

The Healing Power
of Loving-Kindness

A Guided Buddhist Meditation

Tulku Thondup

SHAMBHALA

Shambhala Publications, Inc.
4720 Walnut Street
Boulder, Colorado 80301
www.shambhala.com

© 2008 by Tulku Thondup Rinpoche
This edition published 2021
The Buddhayana Foundation Series XI

Cover art: thangka painting of Avalokiteshvara.
Photograph courtesy of Sotheby's, Inc. © 2006
Cover design: Gopa & Ted2, Inc.
Interior design: Gopa & Ted2, Inc.

9 8 7 6 5 4 3 2 1

First Paperback Edition
Printed in the United States of America

♾ This edition is printed on acid-free paper that meets the American
National Standards Institute z39.48 Standard.
♲ This book is printed on 30% postconsumer recycled paper.
For more information please visit www.shambhala.com.
Shambhala Publications is distributed worldwide by
Penguin Random House, Inc., and its subsidiaries.

LIBRARY OF CONGRESS CATALOGING-IN-PUBLICATION DATA

Names: Thondup, Tulku, author.
Title: The healing power of loving-kindness: a guided Buddhist meditation /
Tulku Thondup. Description: First paperback edition. |
Boulder, Colorado: Shambhala, 2021.| Includes bibliographical references.
Identifiers: LCCN 2020041097 | ISBN 9781611809138
(trade paperback) Subjects: LCSH: Meditation—Buddhism. |
Compassion—Religious aspects—Buddhism. Classification:
LCC BQ5612 .T485 2021 | DDC 294.3/4435—dc23
LC record available at https://lccn.loc.gov/2020041097

Contents

Preface

"LOVING-KINDNESS" (in Sanskrit called *maitri*) is the thought of wishing joy and well-being for all with no selfish attitude. The power of loving-kindness fully awakens our mind and makes it open boundlessly. It is the thought and feeling of unconditional, pure, and universal love—love toward all without any discrimination or distinction, hesitation or reservation, expectation or hope of reward.

A powerful way of awakening loving-kindness in the heart and mind is through connecting to devotion to the Buddha of Loving-Kindness and Compassion (in Sanskrit called Avalokiteshvara). When we talk about devotion, we are talking about opening our heart with great energy, joy, and trust. The joy comes from being in the presence of the Buddha of Loving-Kindness, and the trust is in his unconditional love. As soon as we feel such joy and trust in the Buddha and his unconditional love, we will instantly find our own mind and heart completely steeped in and saturated with the energy of loving-kindness. We feel the qualities of pure love. Such experiences will inspire us to put our pure thoughts and feelings of loving-kindness into action, the words and deeds that reflect loving-kindness for all.

Buddhism teaches that everything we see, hear, or feel originates in the mind, is led by the mind, and is experienced by the mind, or consciousness. In *The Dharmapada,* the Buddha says,

> All are led by the mind.
> Mind is the main factor and it is the forerunner
>   of all actions.
> If one speaks or acts with a pure mind,
> Happiness follows, as a shadow follows its source.[1]

The mind is always preoccupied with mental objects—images, sounds, and sensations. We formulate habits and unending chains of cause and effect within this mind stream, all resulting in either joy or pain. As long as the mind is relating to mental objects with attachment, jealousy, denial, or hatred, our life will be enslaved and conditioned by these mental objects. We will never experience freedom from the up-and-down feelings of sadness, fear, excitement, and pain that we are entrapped in by depending on what's happening from moment to moment in our external environment. Experiences of devotion and loving-kindness, on the other hand, pacify and purify our mental and emotional rigidities and afflictions. They instantly cheer up our heart and awaken the intrinsic pure qualities of our own mind.

Many think that their identity is their body, but from the Buddhist perspective, the mind is who we are and the body is only a temporary resting place for the mind. At death, the body merges into the elements of nature, but the mind migrates into another body, by taking rebirth in accordance with the established habitual tendencies of the mind. Therefore, in order to transform our present life and endless future lives into a state of unconditional love and boundless joy, we must focus on improving the present qualities of the mind, by developing habits of positive thoughts and feelings in our mental stream. This improves the qualities of our mind.

This book and accompanying audio tracks, which can be downloaded at www.shambhala.com/healingpower, offer twelve stages of guided meditations on loving-kindness, along with four meditation tools. The goal of these meditations is to realize three levels of results, in the form of experiences and attainments. The third (visualization of the Buddha of Loving-Kindness) through the fifth (filling the body with the blessing light of loving-kindness) stages are for realizing the first result. The sixth (transforming the body into blessing light and the mind into loving-kindness) through the tenth (sharing the loving-kindness with all) stages are for realizing the second result. The eleventh stage (resting in the awareness of loving-kindness) is for realizing the third result. The first and second stages are the preparatory training for the main stages of meditation, and the twelfth stage is the concluding meditation. The experiences of each set of results are indispensable stepping-stones for enjoying the next results; that is to say, succeeding results are the fruits of the previous ones.

First result: devotion to the Buddha of Loving-Kindness inspires loving-kindness in us. When we are fully perceiving the presence of the Buddha of Loving-Kindness with devotion, and feeling his unconditional love, the quality of our mind changes instantly from negative or neutral thoughts and feelings to positive thoughts and feelings— that is, to loving-kindness. Fully opening our heart in order to experience the amazing joy of being in the presence of the Buddha and having unconditional trust in him and his love is the essence of devotion.

Then we repeat the prayer mantra: OM MANI PADME HUNG. This mantra becomes the sound of the energy waves of our devotion, a force that opens our heart to the Buddha with joy and trust and without any hesitation, reservation, or ego. Seeing and feeling the Buddha's presence and his sacred qualities, such as his unconditional love, generate instant devotion and loving-kindness in our hearts. Our mind and body become boundlessly open with the energy of celebration and confidence.

To attain freedom, we must start by meditating on seeing and feeling the positive qualities of these mental objects. We must meditate on seeing the spiritual qualities of the Buddha of Loving-Kindness in order to generate devotion and loving-kindness in ourselves. If we do so, we will redirect the habits of our mind from a cycle of negative, reactive emotions toward emotions that are positive and loving. We will then spontaneously enjoy a revolutionary transformation in our life. We will gain mental strength and wisdom that bring everlasting freedom from dependence on external circumstances.

This freedom is illustrated in the story of a refugee boy called Pema, who was born and grew up in great poverty. His life was bleak. His joy and suffering were totally at the mercy of others. But eventually, a kind person offered him help, in the form of getting him into a good school. Pema cheerfully and gratefully accepted the assistance. Soon, he started to discover an inexhaustible richness of knowledge and skills within himself, gifts that had in fact been with him all along simply because he was born human. Over time, he not only became joyful and prosperous but was an enriching source of benefit and help for others, too.

Like Pema, the first task we face is that we must dare to open our heart and accept help, in the form of the positive light that comes our way, for our own sake. Seeing and having confidence in the powerful presence of the Buddha of Loving-Kindness and his unconditional love are the beginning of healing and transforming our life. When we experience this devotion to the Buddha of Loving-Kindness—this sense of joy and trust—from the depth of our heart, we will be on our way to enjoying pure thoughts and joyful feelings of love. The ice-like negative emotions and painful sensations of our mind will start melting into the nectar stream of love and joy, because the way that we see the world directly affects what we feel. For example, when someone enters the room, if we perceive him as a terrorist, we will freeze with shock and fear by the mere sight and sound of him. But as soon as we realize that he is a nice and gentle person whom we know well, our heart will be joyous. Likewise, as soon as we see the Buddha as a body of Loving-Kindness, the blazing light of peace, joy, and love will be ignited in our heart, because of the powers of our own pure perception and by the blessed qualities of the Buddha.

If we learn to see any mental object, such as people or nature, ideas or sensations—as a body of positive qualities, then the image, thought, or feeling of loving-kindness will be available for us.

Second result: awakening of the thoughts and feelings of loving-kindness. At the moment of seeing and feeling the unconditional love of the Buddha, all the thoughts in our mind and the feelings of our heart will be changed from negative or neutral states of mind to the mind of loving-kindness. We must recognize this great transformation and celebrate it again and again. Then, we bring others to mind with the feeling of loving-kindness—a strong wish for joy for them—as we have felt the unconditional love of the Buddha ourselves. First we generate loving-kindness and extend that feeling toward one person, someone who invokes loving-kindness in us, such as our mother. Then we meditate on a number of loved ones, then on people about whom we feel neutral, then so-called enemies, and finally on every being in the whole universe.

When our mind becomes a mind of loving-kindness, then all the things we say or do become the words and expressions of loving-kindness. When done in loving-kindness, every activity of our life—talking, cooking, eating, *everything*—sets the wheel of positive karmic deeds in motion. As a result, we will be able to live in authentic peace and happiness, despite whatever is happening around us.

The sound of the mantra OM MANI PADME HUNG, the sound of energy waves of loving-kindness—the opening of our heart with the wish of well-being for all—can change our way of being in the world. As our whole mind and every particle of our body open fully to the Buddha and to all beings—with great joy, the way that flowers blossom in sunlight, smiling at the sun—the whole of existence—images, sounds, and feelings—will turn into the cycle of celebration of great love, of loving-kindness.

Third result: awakening innate loving-kindness, the true nature of the mind. Totally enjoying the Buddha's unconditional love from the depth of our heart and fully opening our mind with loving-kindness will ultimately awaken our own Buddha-nature, the true nature of our mind, as it is. The Buddha said,

> Beings are Buddha in their true nature.
> But their true nature is obscured by temporary afflictions.
> When the afflictions are cleansed, beings are the very Buddha.[2]

When the blessings of Buddha's loving-kindness and the innate loving-kindness of our own mind are united, we have realized universal Buddhahood—blazing with ultimate peace, joy, and loving-kindness.

When the omnipresent loving-kindness of our own mind is awakened and omniscient wisdom is realized, we will have no more conceptual conflicts or emotional afflictions to overcome. We will lose every trace of our tendency toward dualistic concepts, emotional flames, or positive and negative distinctions. The separating boundaries of mind and mental objects will leave with no trace, and our mind instead will feel united with the world—a union of openness and wisdom and boundless love.

The sounds of the prayer—i.e., OM MANI PADME HUNG—will remain as the boundless power of the union of sound and openness. The loving-kindness nature of the mind and its manifestative power remain and illuminate as one union, like the sun and sunlight. The idea that we progress through these three levels of the results of loving-kindness is the true essence of the Buddhist teachings. The interpretations of these teachings here in this book are unique, however.

When we realize any of these three results, we will enjoy the two following benefits, as their fruits.

First benefit: our life turns into a cycle of unconditional love. When the universal loving-kindness has started to develop in our mind, whatever we see, hear, and feel will begin to reflect back to us as images, sounds, and feelings of love. We will see mountains as mountains, walls as walls, and people as people, but instead of seeing them in the form of dark rigidities of emotional and sensational phenomena, we will be able to see all in the light, flavor, quality, and nature of loving-kindness. The external world and the internal mind alike will arise for us as the blazing light of the union of boundless loving-kindness and spacious wisdom.

Second benefit: we become a source of love and joy for others. If we are enjoying loving-kindness in our mind, our physical presence will then become a source of peace, joy, and love for others whose minds are open. Whatever we say or do, even a simple smile, could become a source of heart-warming joy and long-lasting peace for others. Our mere presence could radiate the light and energy of loving-kindness to others in both visible and invisible ways.

If we start our meditation journey of loving-kindness, and if we remain on that path of training, we will spontaneously make progress and will reach the ultimate goal, Buddhahood. This process is not unlike rolling a bowling ball down the lane with proper force and direction so that it will knock down the pins as the result.

These twelve stages of meditation on loving-kindness embody the essence of many other Buddhist meditations, such as those on compassion, devotion, pure perception, contemplation, and the wisdom of awareness of the true nature. If we follow the stages sincerely, we can realize three pivotal results and enjoy two benefits as described above. So, if you are open to joining this journey—a journey along the joyful path to the peaceful goal—you are most welcome to embark on the path of twelve-stage guided meditation on loving-kindness that is detailed in this book.

Acknowledgments

I OFFER my gratitude to Kyala Khenpo Rinpoche and Kyabje Dodrupchen Rinpoche, who are embodiments of loving-kindness, for showing the light of true love. I am grateful to Harold Talbott for editing this text and my other works for the last three decades with wisdom and love. And I wish to thank Lydia Segal—an image of loving-kindness—for reflecting many of these nectarlike teachings.

I am especially thankful to Michael Baldwin for facilitating all the needs of my work with total love and care and likewise thankful to the generous patrons of the Buddhayana Foundation, under whose sponsorship I have been researching for the last twenty-eight years.

I also appreciate Shambhala Mountain Center, Colorado, under whose kind auspices I led a four-day retreat (August 17–20, 2007) on loving-kindness and produced these audio tracks; thank you to Brian Spielman and the other staff of Shambhala Mountain Center for welcoming many to the retreat.

I am deeply grateful to Acharya Samuel Bercholz and Peter Turner of Shambhala Publications for trusting in my work; to Lenny Jacobs for inspiring me to prepare this book; to Gopa & Ted2, Inc. for beautifully designing it; to Hazel Bercholz for overseeing the art direction; and to Jonathan Green and all the Shambhala Publications staff for taking great care of my books.

My special appreciation goes to Acharya Emily Bower for her mastery in the art of editing and Katie Keach for her great skill and dedication in editing the downloadable audio program that accompanies this book.

THE HEALING POWER OF
LOVING-KINDNESS

I

An Introduction to Loving-Kindness

All happiness in the world

Comes from wishing happiness for others.

All suffering in the world

Comes from the desire to have
happiness only for oneself.

—SHANTIDEVA

LOVING-KINDNESS is the thought of wishing joy for all beings and the whole universe—without limits and conditions—and putting that wish into practice. The eighteenth-century Dzogchen teacher Jigme Lingpa wrote, "The essence of loving-kindness is wishing happiness for others. Like a loving mother for her [only] child—It is giving up [your care for] your own body, wealth and [the benefits of] virtuous deeds, and solely serving others and tolerating hardships caused by them."[1] Loving-kindness is love, but it is pure love, love that is totally open, universal, having no limits, unconditional—a love that has no attachment, no ego-centeredness, no self-centeredness.[2]

Meditation on loving-kindness is a training on the thoughts and deeds that benefit others. It is a practice that opens our heart with love to all, causing our life to blossom with feelings of boundless peace and joy.

Peace and joy generated by loving-kindness awaken our own enlightened mind and transform us into skilled, competent, and humble servants for all beings. Authentic world peace and true happiness will only ever come from loving-kindness.

THE BUDDHA OF LOVING-KINDNESS

Traditionally, we start the meditation on loving-kindness by focusing our mind directly on wishing joy for one person and then gradually for others and finally for all. But here, we start the meditation by warming up and opening our devotional heart, by seeing the Buddha as the Buddha of Loving-Kindness (Avalokiteshvara), and then feeling his unconditional love *in us*. When the presence and feeling of the loving-kindness of the Buddha touch us, the loving-kindness of our own mind awakens. Then whatever we see—every being and the whole universe—will arise as the images and feeling of loving-kindness, unconditional love.

Visualizing the Buddha of Loving-Kindness, we think of and feel his unconditional love. Then with prayers we invoke, receive, and enjoy Buddha's love in the form of blessing light. We feel the awakening of the thoughts and feelings of Buddha's pure love in our body, heart, and mind. Such meditation awakens the thoughts and feelings of pure love in us, as the pure love of a loving mother educates her child in true love.

After we have gained some idea and feeling of the loving-kindness of the Buddha, we will go on to see, think of, and feel for other beings through the same feeling of loving-kindness, the wish of joy for all. Then, because of the blessing power of the Buddha of Loving-Kindness, our meditation on loving-kindness will become pure, powerful, and perfect.

Loving-Kindness and Compassion

Avalokiteshvara is popularly known as the Buddha of Compassion. But in fact he is the Buddha of infinite enlightened qualities such as loving-kindness and omniscience, too. That is why we see him as the Buddha of Loving-Kindness. The Shakyamuni Buddha said,

> Pay homage to the lord, Avalokiteshvara
> Who has perfected oceans of virtues,
> Who sees all beings with the eyes of loving-
> kindness and compassion, and
> Whose pure qualities are as vast as the ocean.[3]

When we talk about the Buddha of Loving-Kindness, we are not talking about an individual Buddhist person or figure, but rather we are referring to a symbol, a presence, a quality and source of universal and pure love and blessings, as well as the support for our meditation on loving-kindness.

Meditation on compassion usually starts with thinking about the suffering of others, and aspiring for them not to have suffering and the causes of suffering. Such aspiration always leads us to the realization of great joy, as we are serving others who are in need and realizing that the ultimate compassion is absolute joy, the omnipresence of Buddhahood. However, at the beginning—before reaching the state of such joy—some meditators could be overwhelmed by the thoughts and feelings of the suffering that so many other beings are enduring.

By contrast, meditation on loving-kindness usually starts by aspiring for others to have joy and the causes of joy. For this reason, meditation on loving-kindness may be easier for new meditators, and meditation on loving-kindness and compassion are equally effective trainings. In our practice here, furthermore, we will start the meditation by generating the loving-kindness of the Buddha through the power of our own devotional mind, which is a highly beneficial enhancement of our meditation.

As many of us already know very well, on most occasions the experiences of happiness and suffering in our minds are influenced by how we perceive mental objects—as positive or negative. As I mentioned earlier, if a man enters the room and we perceive him as a terrorist, we will freeze with shock and fear by the mere sight and sound of him. But if we then realize that he is a kind and gentle person whom we know well, we will feel relieved and joyful. If we perceive someone as attractive, we could become attached to that idea of him or her and sleepless obsession could follow. Clearly, how we perceive our mental objects makes a great difference to our mind state and to how we feel and live.

A highly respected lama once told me about his own meditations on loving-kindness and their effects on his life. He was imprisoned for over twenty years, doing hard labor and building roads. He worked laying bricks and putting on roofs six days a week. One might think he would have been unhappy, but he said, "I don't remember being sad or angry even once during all those years. I focused my mind mainly on two meditations. I meditated on compassion, instead of harboring hatred toward our prison guards, because I knew they were accumulating such grave karma by causing pain to so many people that their future lives would be horribly painful.

"I also meditated on joy for the opportunity to be relieved of some of my own karmic debts. The pain that I faced was certainly the result of my own misdeeds in past lifetimes. Now I had the opportunity to exhaust the negative karmas by enduring those consequences. So, it was a joyful time too."

He is such an honest and helpful human being, and a great scholar and meditator, that by the power of his meditation on compassion and joy, therefore, he remained healthy and sane while in prison, and he came out shining with greater peace and joy than before he was imprisoned.

True Loving-Kindness

How and why we love change the qualities of our love. Love with loving-kindness transforms the love into nectar of wisdom. Love with attachment transforms the love into poison, into a state of afflicting emotions. Therefore, we must recognize the characteristics of the love that is loving-kindness and how to generate it in ourselves. Gampopa, one of the greatest masters of the Kagyu school of Tibetan Buddhism, wrote, "The object of the meditation of loving-kindness is all beings. The way is wishing them to have happiness. The formula is thinking about the kindness of beings, since generation of loving-kindness depends on the remembrance of the kindness of beings."[4]

There are three kinds of love—unhealthy love, healthy love, and loving-kindness. Unhealthy love is the love characterized by attachment, by clinging to and craving for any mental object—food, drink, money, ideas, or a person.

Attachment will end up causing obsession, stress, suffocation, sadness, and pain. Healthy love is love characterized by fond and positive thoughts and feelings of caring and appreciation for things, ideas, or loved ones, with less attachment or selfishness. Loving-kindness, however, is unconditional pure love, wishing joy for all others without attachment or selfishness, and this, ultimately, is the kind of love that brings boundless joy, openness, and enlightenment.

In the next chapter, we will start our meditation on loving-kindness by focusing on one person, from the depth of our hearts, so that our meditation will be clear, vivid, heartfelt, and effective. Then, step-by-step, we will expand the thoughts and feelings of loving-kindness to more people and finally to all, to every being, without any limit or discrimination. Otherwise, if we meditate on loving-kindness for all from the beginning, our experience could easily become too vague and intellectual.

Loving-kindness transforms our life. If we have loving-kindness in our mind and heart, we will enjoy authentic peace, joy, and strength. Whatever we say or do will become an expression of that peace and joy—and then, spontaneously, we will become sources of true joy for those who are around us. Experience of peace and joy promotes physical health, because it eases stress, regulates the circulation in the body, and balances the elements of the body—earth, water, fire, and air. Furthermore, loving-kindness generates positive karma, or merit—the cause of happiness and enlightenment.

The Buddha lived on alms, starting the day he assumed an ascetic life at the age of twenty-nine until the day before the Mahaparinirvana, his death, at the age of eighty. He also taught his ordained monks and nuns to live on alms, taking one meal a day, at midday. Before noon, they would go around the town or village and silently stand at the doors of the lay devotees for a minute or so. They would move on to another door if there was no response. They would eat whatever food they were offered, good or bad. They lived in a culture of contentment with simple food and only had their robe and begging bowl for possessions. They saved their time for study and meditation and serving others, instead of hoarding and protecting material goods.

But the greater purpose of living on alms was threefold: (1) For the monks and nuns it was a powerful way of putting compassion and loving-kindness into practice. (2) For the laypeople it was an opportunity to open their hearts with generosity and devotion to the Buddha and his disciples. (3) For the laypeople it was a way of gaining merit; this positive deed is a cause of a joyful rebirth.

The Buddha and his learned disciples offered their lives as vessels for others to gain merit from. According to Buddhism, giving food, the sustenance for life, and especially to those who are a source of peace, wisdom, and benefit for others, is a way of gaining great merit.

The first rule proclaimed by the Buddha for his disciples was not to kill, even the smallest insect. But at the same time, he didn't prohibit monks and nuns from accepting food mixed with meat. The reason was that lower-caste people ate food mixed with meat, and they offered the disciples that food. The Buddha had a special love for lower-caste people and outcasts because they were badly in need of merit to improve their situations.

A Person Is Made of Body and Mind

The body is like a hotel where the mind—that is, consciousness—resides temporarily. At the time of death, mind migrates to another body by taking rebirth in it, like moving to another hotel. Remember that although the body is intimate and precious to us, it is not what we are. Our mind is our identity. And according to Buddhism, if you have lived your life in peace and joy, you are certain to enjoy a rebirth filled with happiness after your death.

Mind as the Source of Loving-Kindness

Material prosperity or social support could help in developing sources of peace and joy, if we are skillful in using them to our advantage. But the real source of these gifts is the mind itself, for loving-kindness is a concept created by the mind. It is an experience felt by the mind. So we must use our own mind to generate loving-kindness in ourselves.

Speaking in simple terms, we can say there are two aspects of the mind: first, the conceptual or ordinary mind; and second, the enlightened mind, that is, intrinsic awareness, or the true nature of the mind. The third Dodrupchen in the Dzogchen lineage, Jigmé Tenpé Nyima, explained, "Mind is the aspect that grasps [mental objects] dualistically and has become the root of samsara. Intrinsic awareness is wisdom, the state of being in the meaning of ultimate nature of all."[5]

Conceptual mind and enlightened mind are not two separate minds, but rather they are two sides of the same coin. The mind is like the ocean, which can be rough on the surface, with mountainous waves stirred up by ferocious winds. But at the bottom it is calm and peaceful.

"Conceptual mind" is the aspect of the mind that we ordinary people are familiar with and employ all the time. It is a stream of consciousness that sees, thinks, and feels mental objects intellectually and emotionally by grasping at them.

We perceive mental objects such as walls, trees, people, ideas, and sensations by grasping at them as truly existing entities. Texts call it grasping at "self." "Self" denotes the concept of a solid, real, and independent entity. As soon as you grasp at the "self," mind and the mental objects break into two, a duality: subjective and objective. That is the starting point of imposing limitations and restrictions on our mental sphere. Then, sticking to those dualistic concepts, the thoughts of discrimination such as "this is a wall," "this is a tree," and so on will arise. From this, the emotions—such as desire, attachment, craving, dislike, hatred—arise, as we think and feel "this is mine," "this is beautiful," "this is bad," and "I hate this."

These emotions produce consequences; they have results. We enjoy various sensations, such as excitement, by obtaining things that we like or by avoiding what we hate, and we experience pain by losing what we want or being subjected to what we hate or suffering disorders in our physical health.

To the extent that the cycle of these discriminations, emotions, and sensations that are rooted in grasping at "self" spins on endlessly, the grip of grasping will be tightened more, and the potential of our mind's peace, joy, and wisdom will be limited. That is how we ordinary beings live and function.

"Enlightened mind," by contrast, is the aspect of the mind that the Enlightened Ones, fully accomplished meditators, have realized. This state of intrinsic awareness is the true nature and quality of our mind. It is supremely peaceful, joyful, and omniscient. Enlightened mind sees all but without grasping at the "self." Because we are not grasping at "self," there is no dividing into duality, no clash and conflict between the rigid surfaces of the mind's dualistic concepts and its mental objects. When we see all with an open mind, we see all in oneness, unity. We see infinite phenomena simultaneously, as a result of the omniscient quality of the mind's nature. Since there are no clashes or conflicts, all is in a state of oneness, a state of ultimate peace, joy, and universal love; all is absolute loving-kindness.

Such a peaceful nature is not only described in Buddhism, it is universal. If you live in a peaceful place or in a situation where you are not bombarded and numbed by encounters with external forces, your mind will become serene, joyful, and wise. In many cases of "near-death experiences," people feel that they are meeting and becoming one with an unexplainable light of sublime bliss. They experience a "life review" in which they view infinite images, sounds, and feelings simultaneously—at an awareness level. All of these examples indicate that the mind has an amazing vastness that most of us are not aware of.

According to the teachings of Buddhism, the true nature of the mind of every being is enlightened. This concept is also called the Buddha-nature, or Buddhahood. If we choose, we can all be Enlightened Ones, Buddhas, by realizing our true nature, as it is, through meditation. Even having that information alone—the understanding that we are all Buddha in our true nature—is a great source of healing, confidence, and courage.

START THE JOURNEY WHERE YOU ARE

In any case, we must each start our meditation journey from wherever we are standing. At this moment, we are functioning with conceptual mind, mind that is grasping at "self" and discriminating between the mental objects and emotions and sensations. What we need to do, and can do in meditation, is to choose images, words, and feelings with positive perceptions and emotions, such as devotion and trust, in order to generate and enjoy positive sensations such as peace and joy. Using positive mental objects, such as images of the Buddha, in the appropriate way, will slowly loosen the tightness of the grip of grasping, ease the stressful experiences of life, and improve our whole life, step-by-step.

Any kind of positive thinking and physical action will become the means of easing grasping, which is the root of all our obsessions, cravings, entrapments, pain, and excitements. Any physical action that causes joy and peace in oneself or others is a positive physical action. This includes giving gifts, protecting lives, serving the sick, observing moral conduct, being tolerant of others, and being industrious. But meditation is the most powerful way to do this. In meditation, if you are doing it properly, your thoughts are focused on the right path from the depth of your heart and the wholeness of your mind.

There are two kinds of meditation. The first is conceptual meditation. In it you train your mind in seeing, thinking, hearing, and feeling positive mental objects in the right way with an organized and disciplined formula. The second is contemplative meditation. In it you train in focusing your mind on an object without wandering. The initial stages of the meditations on loving-kindness given in this book belong to the first approach.

Through meditation such as meditation on loving-kindness, we can not only loosen the tightness of grasping and cause greater peace and joy in ourselves, but we can also help ourselves to reach and realize the enlightened nature of our mind. In meditation, we focus to retune and refine the mind and mental qualities, but we must bring to it our undivided attention and practice from the depth of our heart.

Everything that happens in this life and in successive lives is created by and functions through karmic causations. The right conditions of earth, heat, moisture, air, and seeds cause trees, flowers, and all living things to grow. Positive and negative states of mind, emotions, and actions sow seeds in the deeper, unconscious state of the mind, and these cause happiness or pain in future lives as a result.

Turning negative thoughts into positive ones is essential. Images, words, feelings, and beliefs are the universal means of mental activity. So we must use images, words, and feelings of loving-kindness and we must trust in them if we want to be happy and awaken the ultimate awareness of peace and wisdom, which are the true qualities and nature of our own mind.

And, in order to help others, first we must make ourselves into a proper tool for serving others by improving our own qualities. If our mind is filled with negative emotions, whatever we do will be the expression of those emotions, and therefore, in whomever we reach we could cause ill effects. If we are equipped with loving-kindness, however, even our mere presence could bring authentic peace and joy to those around us. So we must improve our own mental state first, through meditation training.

Four Tools for
Meditation on Loving-Kindness

There are four essential ingredients for meditation on loving-kindness. They are positive images, positive words, feelings of loving-kindness, and trust in these three.

(1) *Loving images.* Any image of positive or pure love, real or visualized, can start to reverse our negative mental attitudes. When we are looking at and seeing a real or visualized image of a person of pure love, or the image of the Buddha of Loving-Kindness, our mind starts to turn from negative thoughts to positive ones. If we can call to mind the positive image and if we can hold the image in mind, that will be very effective because the image has been created and is being maintained by our own mind's contemplative skill. It bears pointing out that all of us always think with images, so visualization is not something from a foreign culture, as some might at first think.

(2) *Loving words.* Labeling the image that you are seeing with loving and positive words, and returning to the image if your mind wanders, again and again, will make the image a powerful source of inspiration and improve your life. We always think with words, so using positive words in this way is just bringing a familiar activity to our meditation. If we could convert the treasury of our lexicon into positive words—such as words of loving-kindness— our life would certainly be improved.

(3) *Loving feeling.* It is important to enjoy the qualities of images and words of pure love at the level of your heart by

feeling them—instead of just seeing and thinking of them at the intellectual and external level. Feeling the positive qualities of the mental objects—such as the pure love of a kind person and love of the Buddha—is a powerful means of transforming our life at a deeper heart level.

(4) *Trusting in love.* Trusting in the power of images, words, and feelings of loving-kindness makes our meditation on loving-kindness more effective. Trust might be hard to come by for many of us, but liking the images, words, and feelings of loving-kindness is the beginning of trust. Trust is based upon the knowledge and conviction that the power of loving-kindness can be fully called forth with the help of loving images of, and words and feelings about, a loving person or the Buddha of Loving-Kindness.

Applying the Four Tools of Loving-Kindness

How do we apply these four meditation tools? We must use them in the right way. Even if we are seeing and feeling the image of the Buddha of Loving-Kindness, if we make that image into an object and a means of tightening mental grasping, attachment, craving, obsession, or hatred, then our interaction with the image will only cause negative consequences. So we must see, think of, and feel the positive object as the means of opening our mental views, emotional passions, sensory feelings, and even physical energy—and causing those to blossom. If we do that, then we will create openness, peace, joy, and loving-kindness as the result.

2

The Twelve Stages of Guided Meditation

on

Loving-Kindness

THE FOLLOWING twelve-stage meditation on loving-kindness should be practiced together with the four meditation tools that we just discussed. Before you begin the stages, here are a few points to keep in mind:

Posture: You can meditate by sitting on a cushion with crossed legs, or by sitting on a chair, or even lying on a bed if necessary. In this particular meditation, whatever position helps you to feel comfortable will be best. However, keep your spine straight, so the main channels and arteries of your body will be aligned. Then your breathing will become normal and your mind will function with ease.

Breathing: Breathe normally, naturally, with ease. Don't hold or restrict your breathing one way or another. If necessary, you could breathe with the mouth slightly open.

Eyes: You can meditate with eyes open or closed. With eyes open is better because it brings more light and wakefulness into the meditation; alternatively, with eyes closed is easier for visualizing because images in your environment won't distract you.

For meditation, the most important things are to be relaxed, awake, and to feel open. On the accompanying downloadable audio program (see www.shambhala.com/healingpower), I lead a loving-kindness meditation. While the twelve stages are laid out chronologically in the book, the actual practice can be more fluid, as I demonstrate.

STAGE ONE—
DEVELOP THE RIGHT ATTITUDE

Before starting the main meditation, we should develop the right attitude, an enlightened attitude. With strong loving-kindness for all, imagine and feel from the depth of your mind and heart, "I am going to meditate on loving-kindness for the benefit of all beings, infinite as space."

With such strong intention and aspiration, embark on the following meditations. If you practice with the intention of helping yourself, the meditation will become meritorious and helpful. But if you practice with the intention of benefiting all beings, the scope and force of your meditation power will become vast and boundless. Then, according to Buddhism, the merit or good karma of your practice will certainly benefit others, along with yourself, enormously.

Stage Two—
Bring the Mind Back to the Body

Mind is the main factor and leader of all the activities and experiences of our life. That is why the Buddha said, "Mind is the forerunner of all things."[1] The body is the closest companion, foundation, and anchor, the most vital vessel, for our mind and life as long as we are alive. In order to improve our life, then, we must find a way to help our mind and body to work together in union, as one team.

Unfortunately, for many of us the relationship between mind and body has become, to use a relationship term, "dysfunctional." During sleep, body and mind are more or less together, but mostly they are in a semiconscious state. As soon as we awaken, our mind flies away like an escapee and only communicates with the body by sending endless messages telling the body what it wants. Mind might send a message saying, "I'd like to have a cup of coffee." The body eagerly, or reluctantly, waddles to the kitchen, makes a cup of coffee, and swallows it down in order to please the mind. There is no intimacy between them, very little harmonious thinking, hardly any appreciation of each other, and almost no genuine communication is going on. In many ways, they don't know each other and don't even seem to wish to. At the same time, mind is very much attached to and protective of the body and will do anything to guard it from unwanted pain or discomfort. The energy of such an unhealthy relationship only causes suffocation, strangling, stress, and even abuse and pain.

That is the reason we must acknowledge our situation and recognize the importance of the mind-and-body relationship. We need to focus on improving the relationship by applying the first three of our four meditation tools: seeing positive images, thinking compassionate thoughts, and feeling positive perceptions in both body and mind—with openness and receptivity, not tightness—as we discussed earlier.

Focusing on Peace and Calm

Whatever you think and whatever you say, all of your thoughts and words make a great impact. As the Buddha said, "You are what you think." With a relaxed mind, go through the following steps.

First think that all the tension in your mind has left you. Then tell yourself, and imagine and feel, that your body is filled with peace and calm. All the feelings of your body have transformed into the feeling of peace and calm. Just focus your mind on the feeling of peace and calm, and enjoy it, returning to the feeling repeatedly if your mind wanders.

Then focus your mind on the feeling of peace and calm

in your head, and enjoy it, returning to the feeling again and again. Then focus your mind on the feeling of peace and calm in your upper body, and enjoy it. Then focus your mind on the feeling of peace and calm in your arms and hands, and enjoy that, always returning to the feeling if your mind wanders. Then, focus your mind on the feeling of peace and calm in your lower body, and enjoy that. Then focus your mind on the feeling of peace and calm in your legs and feet, and enjoy that. Then focus your mind on the feeling of peace and calm in every particle (or cell, if you prefer) of your body, and enjoy that feeling. Then focus your mind on the feeling of peace and calm in your whole body, and enjoy it.

Then focus your mind on the feeling of peace and calm in the room where you are sitting, and enjoy the feeling, returning repeatedly to the feeling in the room if your mind wanders. Then focus your mind on the feeling of peace and calm in the things and people in the room where you are sitting, and enjoy that. Then focus your mind on the feeling of peace and calm in the valley (or city, or area), where you are, and enjoy that.

Then focus your mind on the sounds that you hear in your environment—the sounds of nature, birds, people, breathing, traffic, wind, and so on. Think of and feel these sounds as the vibrations of peace and calm in your environment, whether they are sounds of the natural world, of people, of traffic, or of wind, and enjoy the energy waves of peace, returning to them again and again.

This meditation slowly brings the thoughts and feelings of peace to your body, and as soon as you are feeling peace in your body, your mind starts becoming peaceful and calm—because, in reality, your mind is initiating those thoughts of peace and calm, and your mind is enjoying the feeling of peace and calm. In turn, when your mind is peaceful and calm, whatever you see, hear, and feel becomes peaceful and calm. Then both your mind and body are relaxing and uniting in peace and calm.

Anchoring the Mind in the Body

First remember that you are sitting on your seat—on a cushion or a chair. Then focus your mind on the feeling, just the feeling of your body touching your seat. In a relaxed way, keep focusing your mind on the feeling of your body touching the seat.

Then remember that you are sitting on the ground, the earth—directly or indirectly. Focus on the feeling of your body touching the earth. Then remember the qualities of Mother Earth. The earth is firm, solid, strong, immovable, unshakable. Focus your mind on the feeling of your body touching and experiencing the earth's qualities and energies.

Then imagine and feel that your body is being filled up

with earth energies—the energies of heaviness, firmness, and solidity. Earth energies are filling up your feet, legs, lower body, upper body, arms and hands, and head—up to the crown of the head. Your body has become a body of union, the union of peace that you have already been experiencing, with strength, the qualities of the earth you are experiencing now. Enjoy the union of peace and strength, returning again and again to the feeling if your mind wanders.

Finally, relax in the awareness of peace, ultimate peace. Your body and mind are in union, union in the awareness of peace and strength. Awareness of anchoring in peace is the greatest source of joy and all the positive aspects of mind. If you are peaceful, you become a source of peace and joy for others.

These exercises will unite your mind and body in the union of peace and strength. They anchor your mind in your body and your body on the seat, which connects you to the earth.

Stage Three—Visualize the Buddha of Loving-Kindness

With your mind's eye, visualize a totally vast, open, and immaculate sky in front of you. There are no clouds, mountains, or ocean, but only deep and clear blue sky.

Look around; there are no limits or boundaries to the sky, it is boundless. Now appreciate it with positive words or thoughts. How clear and open this amazing sky is! How boundless and spacious it is! How beautiful it is! Then enjoy the feeling of the positive qualities of the sky in you. Feel the immaculate quality of the sky in you. Feel the spaciousness and boundless qualities of the sky in you. Fully open your heart to the pure and clear qualities of the sky and enjoy them, returning to that feeling again and again.

As your mind is projecting and feeling the qualities of the sky, if you let your mind enjoy and feel the feelings of the pure sky, soon the qualities of your mind will transform into the pure open qualities of the sky.

Now, in the middle of the vast and pure sky, visualize a huge flower. It is huge like a mountain. It is radiant and luminous as if it is made of rainbow light. It is colorful and fresh with dewdrops. Millions and billions of its petals are fully open and blossoming. Keep looking at the amazing flower again and again. Then appreciate the beauty and qualities of the flower. Feel the fresh and radiant qualities of the blossoming flower in your mind and body, returning to the feeling again and again if your mind wanders. Fully open your heart and inhale and enjoy the qualities of the flower.

Then, on top of the flower, visualize a disk-shaped seat cushion that is made of light and radiates that soft light, like the moon. This is traditionally called a moon seat, or moon cushion. This moon cushion is made of white light. It is clear, pure, shining, and radiant. The moon cushion covers two-thirds of the top of the flower. Keep looking at the amazing moon cushion. Appreciate and enjoy the beauty and clarity, the shining and pure quality of the moon cushion. Fully open your heart, and inhale and enjoy the qualities of the moon cushion, again and again.

Then on the throne of the giant flower and moon cushion, visualize the presence of the Buddha of Loving-Kindness and Compassion—Avalokiteshvara.[2] His presence fills the greater part of the sky in front of you.

His body is a body of white light, as if made of rainbow light. It is radiant, luminous, translucent, and intangible.[3] He is said to be transparent, not solid, so we can see through him, although we see him vividly. The purpose of seeing him this way is to let go of our habits and concepts of seeing, of taking objects to be real and solid and concrete. When we train by seeing images as insubstantial, our own mental perceptions will start to be more flexible and more open. This is a stepping-stone that leads to the state of blossoming and opening fully into a state of nonduality.

His body is so large that it is as if his head is touching the sky. All these qualities symbolize the purity and boundless quality of the Buddha. His complexion is white and shining, as if it is a crystal mountain touched by the light of thousands of suns, to symbolize his immaculate Buddha qualities. He is wearing princely attire made of fine silk and brocades of light. He is adorned with ornaments and a crown of precious jewels, to symbolize the spiritual richness of the enlightened qualities of the Buddha.

He is sitting firmly in meditative posture on the moon cushion to symbolize that the Buddha always remains in a state of evenness without wavering and changing.

He has four arms. The palms of his first two hands are joined together at his heart to symbolize the union, the oneness, of samsara and nirvana in their true nature. This gesture teaches that in Buddha there is no discrimination or distinction of good and bad. All are one. Between the palms of his first two hands he holds a wish-fulfilling jewel, to symbolize his wish-fulfilling compassion and loving-kindness. His second right hand holds a rosary, or *mala,* of crystal beads, to symbolize that Buddha's loving-kindness never ends. In his second left hand, he holds a white lotus by the stem, to symbolize that Buddha's omniscient wisdom is unstained.

He is youthful, as if sixteen years old, as the Buddha is beyond aging and decay. His fresh, blossoming face is filled with a smile of joy, as there is not even a trace of sorrow in him. His beautiful eyes have the softness of a deer's and they are looking at you directly as his omniscient wisdom sees all directly, distinctively, and simultaneously. His loving eyes are looking at you without blinking, to symbolize that he is looking at and caring for you with unconditional love with no interruption. His body is surrounded by auras, colorful rings of light. Rays of blessing light from his body are being emitted in all directions, illuminating the darkness everywhere as his blessings reach all.

The enlightened mind of the Buddha of Loving-Kindness has three major qualities. See, remember, and feel them by meditating on each of the following:

His omniscient wisdom sees all things as they appear and knows their true nature as it is. He sees all the beings and all the events that occur in the universe, and he sees them simultaneously. He sees all the details of every particle of your body clearly. He sees all the details of your body and everything that occurs in your mind vividly. He sees your past, your present, and your future with perfect clarity. And he sees all the details of the lives of every being, and all the details of the whole universe. He knows all your needs and how to fulfill them.

His pure and unconditional love and compassion manifest as his care for every person as his only child. He is in touch with and caresses every particle of your body and all aspects of your mind with his boundless and universal love. He cares for every being and for the whole universe with his unconditional and boundless love.

His limitless blessing power fulfills the needs of every being simultaneously, the needs of whomever is open. If you keep the doors and windows of your room closed, the sunlight will have no chance to come in, but as soon as you open them, the room will be filled with the light of the sun. Likewise, if your mind is open, Buddha's blessing power will always be ready to come in to fulfill your wishes.

After reflecting on these qualities, feel the presence of the Buddha of Loving-Kindness:

Feel the warmth and comfort of the presence of the Buddha, as if you are sitting by a fire in freezing winter. The coldness and frozen mentality and emotions that you harbor in your mind cause frigidity, sadness, and hopelessness. Feel now that they are melted and dissolved by the warmth of the Buddha's presence.

Feel the security of the presence of the Buddha. Now you have the Buddha's omniscient wisdom, unconditional love, and boundless power with you, as your source of blessing and support; he is your protector and friend. There is no reason for you to feel fear or loneliness. In the presence of the Buddha, the ultimate protector, all the feelings of fear, loneliness, vulnerability, insecurity, and injury that you endure have disappeared and vanished from the depth of your consciousness. Not even a trace of them is left behind.

Feel fulfilled and nurtured by the presence of the Buddha. In the presence of the Buddha of wisdom, love, and power, all your needs are fulfilled, nothing is lacking. Now even if you are sick, poor, or dying, nothing will make you feel lacking or unhappy, as you have found the ever-present Buddha of wisdom, love, and power in yourself, in your life, and in all.

Recognize and remember the identity of Buddha: the Buddha of Loving-Kindness is not just a Buddhist person. He is the embodiment of all the Enlightened Ones, the Buddhas, bodhisattvas, saints, sages, and enlightened masters.

He is not an individual, separate from other beings. He is the manifestation of the pure nature and qualities of the whole universe in the form of the Buddha of Love.

Most important, he is not someone else. He is the reflection of the enlightened nature and qualities of your own mind, which is appearing in front of you in the form of the Buddha of Loving-Kindness. If you look into a mirror, you will see your own face looking back at you. Likewise, the reflection of the loving-kindness of your own mind appears in the form of the Buddha of Loving-Kindness in front of you. So if you meditate on seeing and feeling the Buddha of Loving-Kindness, the loving-kindness of your own heart will be awakened, strengthened, refined, and perfected into ultimate and universal love.

Who is seeing and feeling the Buddha of Loving-Kindness? Your mind is seeing and feeling it. When you are able to see the presence of the Buddha of Loving-Kindness in front of you, and if you allow yourself to feel and enjoy it as such, your mind is waking up to the thoughts and feelings of loving-kindness. The enlightened nature of your mind is starting to manifest its fundamental qualities. And when your mind becomes the mind of loving-kindness, all the images that you see, such as mountains, trees, and people, will spontaneously become images of loving-kindness for you. All the sounds that you hear and all the feelings that you experience will spontaneously become the sounds and feelings of loving-kindness for you. Then, in turn, the absolute nature and pure qualities of your own mind—ultimate peace, love, and wisdom—will be reflected again, as the Buddha of Loving-Kindness in front of you, like the shining moon reflecting in a beautiful pond. So, if you realize it, the Buddha of Loving-Kindness is in you and in all.

The presence of the Buddha in front of you—to whom you prayed and from whom you received blessings—is like a key to open up your mind, so that you can be awakened as the all-pervading, universal Buddha of Loving-Kindness.

Thus, you can see the Buddha of Loving-Kindness as the embodiment of infinite Enlightened Ones. Or if you prefer, you could visualize infinite Enlightened Beings in the sky around the Buddha of Loving-Kindness, like a huge assembly. They have bodies of light in various postures, costumes, and activities; they have minds of wisdom, love, and power. They are all looking at you with unconditional love and care. Feel the love and care of infinite powerful Enlightened Ones, all the time.

Again, return to and refresh your visualization of the amazingly beautiful and luminous body of light of the Buddha. Enjoy the loving eyes of the Buddha and his youthful, clear, and radiant face filled with the smile of joy and peace. Feel the unconditional love, omniscient wisdom, and boundless power of the Buddha. And enjoy the warmth, security, and fulfillment of the presence of the Buddha, again and again.

STAGE FOUR—
PRAY WITH DEVOTION TO THE BUDDHA

Sing and chant the six-syllable prayer (or mantra) of the Buddha of Loving-Kindness—OM MANI PADME HUNG—to pray for, to call, and to invoke the loving-kindness of the Buddha.

Buddha doesn't need our prayers. He sees all through his omniscience, and his loving-kindness is with each of us all the time. But if prayer is offered from the depth of your heart and with the totality of your mind, with the power of devotional energies, it forcefully opens the eyes of your own mind to see and enjoy the qualities and the blessings of the Buddha. Such prayers dismantle all the walls and fortifications of your mental doubts, hesitations, and resistance that you have erected within you and around you to incarcerate yourself. If you open your mind with the power of peace and joy, you will attain freedom from limitations. So, like a child calling to parents for love, care, and help, pray to the Buddha of unconditional love for yourself and for all.

The main focus of this prayer is not to worship an external image or power for support; the purpose rather is to open your own positive mental views and feelings. This blossoming of positive emotional energies, through the power and skills of your own mind, opens to and invites all phenomena as a source of peace, joy, and blessing.

Think about how the world is filled with all kinds of beings—human beings, animals, visible beings, and invisible beings of the six realms. The hearts of all are open with the energy of devotion to the Buddha of Ultimate Love. The faces of all beings are blossoming with smiles of joy, the joy of being in the presence of the Buddha of Ultimate Love. Their eyes are wide open with great amazement from seeing the radiant Buddha of pure love. Infinite beings of the universe are joining with you in the absolute prayer from the heart. Every sound of the world—the sounds of wind, sounds of nature, sounds of people, sounds of traffic, and sounds of breathing—is the sound of the vibration of devotional prayers; devotion to the Buddha of Ultimate Love. The whole universe is filled with the beautiful sounds of prayer, like the musical sounds filling a symphony hall. Imagine and feel that your heart and mind and the hearts and minds of all beings are opening and blossoming with the energy of devotion. The whole universe is opening with the energy of devotion to the Buddha of Ultimate Love.

And now, chant the six-syllable prayer[4] of the Buddha of Loving-Kindness in a traditional melody, or create your own inspiring melody, with total trust and devotion in the Buddha. As the nineteenth-century Tibetan Buddhist master Paltrul Rinpoche advised,

> The unfailing, perpetual sources of refuge are
>   the Three Jewels.
> The embodiment of the Three Jewels is
>   Avalokiteshvara.
> With unwavering trust and devotion to him
> Recite the six-syllables with confidence and resolve.[5]

Repeat the six-syllable prayer—tens, hundreds, thousands, hundreds of thousands of times or more:

Om Ma-Ni Pad-Me Hung (Hoong)

Each element of the six-syllable prayer is rich with meaning:

Om: A + O + M = Om: Enlightened Speech + Body + Mind = Buddha. Or O.

Mani: Jewel: Skillful Means—Loving-kindness and compassion that fulfill the needs and wishes of all.

Padme: Lotus: Wisdom—Emptiness and openness, the undefiled primordial purity.

Hung: Seed syllable of the Buddha: Enlightened Mind. Unity of wisdom and skillful means. *Hung* is also the unity of the five primordial wisdoms of Buddhahood. Or it is for invoking Buddha's blessings.

A simple translation of the six-syllable prayer is: "O Buddha of jewel (loving-kindness) and lotus (wisdom), please grant us/me your blessings."

While chanting the six-syllable prayer at different stages of the meditation, we generate different meditative thoughts and experiences. First, we use the prayer— the sound of the vibration of devotional energies from our heart to the Buddha—to open and make our own heart and mind blossom with great joy and celebration. Then we feel that every sentient being is opening and celebrating with the warmth of devotional energy, the way flowers blossom with the touch of sunlight. The chill of sadness and stress and anxiety that brings us down is melted, and our mind and body are able to open and awaken with bliss because of this warmth, the heat from energy that is generated by devotion to and trust in the Buddha. Then we imagine that the whole of existence— images, sounds, and feelings—transforms into images, sounds, and feelings of devotional prayers. Finally, we imagine that the sound of devotional energy has reached the Buddha and has invoked the presence of his unconditional love. As a result, the Buddha is ready to send his blessings, and we are fully open and ready to receive them.

STAGE FIVE— RECEIVE THE BLESSINGS

Visualize and believe that you are receiving infinite beams of blessing light of loving-kindness in various colors emitted from the Buddha's body—especially from his forehead, mouth, and heart—fulfilling your wishes, as Shakyamuni Buddha said,

Projecting immeasurable colorful lights [from his body],

[Amitabha] fulfills the wishes of beings, as they wish.[6]

First you receive the blessings, and later you share them with others.

Blessing Light

Blessing light has the form of beautiful, luminous, and pure streams of light of various colors, like rainbow light. These multiple rainbow-colored streams of light are the pure qualities of the five elements—white light of water, yellow of earth, red of fire, green of air, and blue of space. The third Dodrupchen says, "You must think that the lights of white, red, blue, and other colors are as the nectar-of-bliss appearing in the form of light."[7]

Moisture in the light is the water element. In meditation, if it is appropriate for you, you could focus on feeling the blessing light as a stream of radiant nectar that can heal and nurture you or wash away all impurities.

Stability, solidity, and heaviness in the light are the earth element. You could focus on feeling the qualities of solidity, firmness, and heaviness of the light to feel yourself strengthened, to anchor yourself and calm down.

Heat and burning qualities of the light are the fire element. You could focus on feeling the warmth and brightness of the light in order to grow, energize, and glow or, alternatively, to burn away impurities.

The qualities of mobility and lightness of the light are the air element. You could focus on feeling the mobility and lightness to change, to move, and to elevate, or to sweep or blow away impurities.

The qualities of openness, boundlessness, and spaciousness of the light are the space element. You could focus on the feeling of the openness and boundlessness of the light to relax, release, open, and liberate.

This blessing light possesses blessing energies of blissfulness and heat—that is, blissful heat. Most of the mental, emotional, and physical ills that we endure are rooted in sadness, loneliness, fear, pain, and feelings of coldness and frozenness. It is essential, then, to enjoy the blessing light as a light having heat and bliss—or warmth and joy, if you prefer.

These beams of blessing light can also be looked upon as representations of Buddha's omniscient wisdom, which sees and knows all simultaneously. They are manifestations of Buddha's unconditional love, which embraces and cares for each and every being as his only child. They are manifestations of Buddha's boundless power, which protects and fulfills the wishes and needs of each and every being. In fact, the blessing light is the very presence of the Buddha himself.

Healing and Purifying All the Ills of Life

Visualize and feel that infinite beams of blessing light with blessing energies—blissful heat—enter you through every pore of your body. See and feel that the beams of blessing light, with blissful heat and wisdom, the love and power of the Buddha, fill every particle of your body. They are purifying, healing, strengthening, and opening. They cause your mind and body to blossom.

Feel that the light of omniscient wisdom of the Buddha is seeing and touching every particle of your body, as the light of the sun touches everything without any distinction.

Feel and enjoy the light of the unconditional love of the Buddha. Imagine that it is touching and caressing every particle of your body, like a loving mother touches her only child, or as sunlight touches every part of the earth— high and low, rich and poor, ugly and beautiful. Enjoy that universal, pure, and boundless love of the Buddha, like the warmth of the sun nurturing the flowers and making them blossom.

Feel and believe that the light of the boundless power of the Buddha's loving-kindness is touching and empowering every particle of your body. Feel the amazing power, strength, and force of the blessing light in you, for now it is in your body and mind.

Feel that the stream of light of blessing energies of Buddha's loving-kindness fills your whole body. With its touch, it melts, loosens, and washes away the tight grip of grasping in your mind; it erases all craving and obsessive emotions. Imagine that it melts all the cold and frozen feelings in the depth of your heart, and all the sadness, fear, pain, and loneliness in your mind and body. Then your body is filled with the stream of nectar-of-light, glowing with blissful heat, generating warmth, peace, joy, strength, and boundless loving-kindness.

Your body is flooded and filled by the stream of light, the light of the pure qualities of the five elements. The light of the water element with moisture and fluidity, like nectar, has washed away your mental and physical ills, toxicities, tumors, and pain without leaving any trace behind. Then your body is filled with the stream of nectar-of-light, with blissful heat, healing your ills and nurturing your body and mind, restoring the decay of your body and mind back to health.

The light of the earth element with solidity and weight rids you of all the unstable and weak mental and physical energies; it strengthens, empowers, and anchors your body and mind in peace and calm.

The light of fire with heat eliminates coldness, darkness, and sadness; it infuses your body and mind with passion, heat, and vigor.

The light of the air element blows away the dead, sinking, and low energies as well as the filth and impurities in your mind and body; it promotes the wind of vital force and waves of inspiring energies.

The light of space clears out all the constricting, limiting, and restricting forces of your body and mind; it opens everything in your experience as boundless, creating multiple dimensions and possibilities.

Your body is filled with the stream of light of wisdom, love, and power of the Buddha. It softens, loosens, melts or washes, and sweeps away all your grasping concepts and negative emotions—the causes of all the ills of life—without leaving any residue behind in your body. As soon as all the impurities are washed out of your body, they evaporate into thin air without leaving any trace. The impurities, tumors, blockages, toxicities, and ills of your body are washed away by the flood of nectar and are swept away by the broom of blessing light totally and completely.

All sadness, fear, loneliness, pain, and confusion, in the form of darkness, is dispelled by the power of the amazingly bright light of wisdom, love, and power of the Buddha. All impurities are washed away by the force of the stream of blessing light. Finally, your body becomes clean and completely filled with the light of Buddha's omniscient wisdom, unconditional love, and boundless power.

STAGE SIX—
TRANSFORMATION
OF YOUR BODY AND MIND

Now, imagine and feel that not only have your body and mind been purified and healed, but your body has transformed into a body of blessing light filled with blessing energies—blissful heat. Your body is no longer a body of flesh, blood, and bones covered by skin, but rather it is a body made of colorful and luminous light, amazingly bright and radiant—as in reality, the gross elements are truly made of lights of different colors.[8] Your body is pure, clear, translucent, radiant, and intangible. Feel the pure and radiant qualities of your body. Now there is no faculty in your body for stress or pressure, since your body has become a body of intangible light.

Your mind has transformed into a mind of all-knowing wisdom, unconditional love, and boundless power of the Buddha. There is no room in you for sadness, fear, or negative thoughts and emotions, since your mind has become the mind of love, wisdom, and power of the Buddha. Feel the enlightened qualities again and again.

Then see and feel that your body is made of billions and trillions of particles (or cells). Each particle is a particle of light, luminous and radiant and blossoming, like flowers of light. Each particle is boundless, like seeing and feeling outer space. Each particle is filled with the blissful heat, omniscient wisdom, unconditional love, and boundless power of the Buddha.

First, see and feel that your head is made of billions of particles. Each particle is a particle of light with luminous and radiant qualities. Every particle is boundless and limitless like space. Every particle is a particle of light of loving-kindness filled with the energies of blissful heat. Each particle is a particle of unconditional love with the omniscient wisdom and boundless power of the Buddha. Then enjoy the body of luminous and boundless qualities filled with blissful heat and loving-kindness of the Buddha.

See and feel that your upper body is made of billions of particles. Each particle is a particle of light—luminous, radiant, and boundless. Each particle is filled with blissful heat and the light of loving-kindness of the Buddha. Then enjoy the body of luminous and boundless qualities filled with the blissful heat and loving-kindness of the Buddha.

See and feel that your arms and hands are made of billions of particles. Each particle is a particle of light—luminous, radiant, and boundless. Each particle is filled with blissful heat and the light of loving-kindness of the Buddha. Then enjoy the body of luminous and boundless qualities filled with the blissful heat and loving-kindness of the Buddha.

See and feel that your lower body is made of billions of particles. Each particle is a particle of light—luminous, radiant, and boundless. Each particle is filled with blissful heat and the light of loving-kindness of the Buddha. Then enjoy the body of luminous and boundless qualities filled with the blissful heat and loving-kindness of the Buddha.

See and feel that your legs and feet are made of billions of particles. Each particle is a particle of light—luminous, radiant, and boundless. Each particle is filled with blissful heat and the light of loving-kindness of the Buddha. Then enjoy the body of luminous and boundless qualities filled with the blissful heat and loving-kindness of the Buddha.

Then see and feel that your whole body is made of trillions of particles. Each particle is a particle of light—luminous, radiant, and boundless. Each particle is filled with blissful heat and the light of loving-kindness of the Buddha. Then enjoy the luminous body of boundless qualities filled with the blissful heat and loving-kindness of the Buddha.

Especially, feel the presence of the Buddha of Loving-Kindness in your own heart center—the center of your body and your feelings. He is radiating a boundless body of light—the light of unconditional love and omniscient wisdom filling your body and all beings with blissful heat. This is the main source of your blessings of loving-kindness for others.

In brief, your body has become a boundless radiant

body of light, emitting rays of light with love and bliss-ful heat. There is no room for darkness, chilliness, pain, or negative emotions in your body, mind, or the atmosphere.

Finally, see and feel that your mind—the subject; your body—the object; and loving-kindness—the action, all three have become joined in the union of awareness of unconditional love. Enjoy the awareness feelings of the unity of your open mind, infinite body, and unconditional love.

Stage Seven— Blessing-Energy Waves

Blessing-energy waves of loving-kindness are the power-ful waves of movement that travel throughout your body. Waves of energy carry the different elements: the weight, firmness, and strength of earth; the moisture and saturation of water; the heat and vigor of fire; the lightness and mobil-ity of air; and the openness and boundlessness of space.

When we meditate on the waves of blessing energies of loving-kindness, we transform the powerful, but passive, blessing energies experienced in meditation stages five and six into an active energy force that purifies, heals, and awakens our body and mind.

First, imagine that your body is breathing from your abdomen, up through the respiratory system. Take deep breaths and focus your mind on the movements of breathing, the waves of loving-kindness. If your mind wanders, return to this feeling of the breathing.

Then imagine that all and every boundless particle of light of your body—filled with blessing energies of loving-kindness—is breathing. While exhaling, imagine and feel that each boundless particle of your body is sending waves of blissful heat with the unconditional love of the Buddha to others, as offerings, with respect and love. While inhaling, imagine and feel that every boundless particle of light of your body is receiving waves of blissful heat of loving-kindness from others, with respect and love. Feel the waves of loving-kindness with blissful heat in and between the boundless particles of your body of light.

Imagine and feel that every part of your body has connected and linked as one body with the energy stream. Every particle is blossoming with radiance without sickness or decay. Every particle is filled with blissful heat. Every particle is blossoming and sending waves of loving-kindness. All the veins and arteries are open, and blessing-energy waves are flowing through them. Every particle of your body is active and all are participating and working as one team—with blessing energies of openness, blissfulness, luminosity, boundlessness, and unconditional love of the Buddha.

If you like, you could include these breathing exercises, which are known to help balance the heart rate and the nervous system. First, with mind and breath in sync, inhale a little slower than usual, and gently fill your belly with the breath, the blessing-energy waves. Then, hold the breath for second a or so, and exhale, a little slower than usual, fully emptying your chest and abdomen of breath. Repeat this exercise a few times, as is comfortable.

Finally, enjoy the subtle awareness of the waves—of the unity of your mind, the subject; your body, the object; and the waves, the action—the loving-kindness.

When and if you feel any pressure in your mind or body while doing this meditation, relieve it by remembering the qualities of your meditative body—made of intangible light and boundless openness and unconditional love.

STAGE EIGHT— ## THE SOUND OF BLESSING-ENERGY WAVES

Every movement has a sound. If you meditate on the sounds of the blessing-energy waves of loving-kindness, the waves will become even more powerful and effective.

We could use the positive sound of any phrase, such as a prayer like OM MANI PADME HUNG or a word that you like. But, here, we use the sound of AH. In both esoteric and common Buddhist teachings, AH has been praised as the most sacred and powerful sound. As space provides room for all matter and all living beings of the universe, AH is known as the source of all sounds, and in every sound there is an AH. However, AH doesn't impose any conceptual designation and limitation. It is boundless, limitless, and infinite. AH is therefore known as the sound of emptiness, openness, the unborn, and the ultimate nature of all. The Buddha gave teachings known as "The Perfection of Wisdom in One Hundred Thousand Verses" (the Prajnaparamita Sutras), but he said that if you condense the teachings they become one syllable, AH. Also, at a simple level, AH has the quality of being universal and nondenominational.

When you exhale, sing the sound of AH: "Ahhhhh." When you inhale, you can't sing with sound, but sing AH in your mind's voice: "Ahhhhh." While exhaling, imagine and feel that each boundless particle of your body is sending waves of blissful warmth and unconditional love of the Buddha, with the sound of AH: "Ahhhhh." While inhaling, imagine and feel that every boundless particle of light of your body is receiving waves of blissful warmth and unconditional love, with the sound of AH: "Ahhhhh." Try to hear the vibrations of the waves in and between the boundless particles of your body of light of loving-kindness: "Ahhhhh."

All the particles of your body are active and working as one team—with the force of energy, blissfulness, luminosity, boundlessness, and unconditional love of the Buddha with the sound of AH: "Ahhhhh."

Finally, enjoy the awareness of the sound waves and the waves of the unity of your mind, the subject; your body, the object; and the waves of sound, the action—loving-kindness.

STAGE NINE—OFFERING LOVING-KINDNESS TO A LOVED ONE

According to the teachings of Buddhism, if you offer meditation and merit to others, they will benefit and your own meditative power and merit will increase as well, because the meditation of offering to others itself is a great source of merit.

Before offering or sharing the blessings, we ourselves must gain meditation experience and receive blessings. So now, if you have achieved the meditations of the first eight stages effectively, the time has come to put the meditation on loving-kindness—wishing joy for others—into action and service.

In order to make the images and feelings of the meditation vivid, thorough, and effective—from the depth of your heart—at the beginning, you must meditate on loving-kindness toward just one person. The ultimate goal of your practice will be to develop strong loving-kindness toward every being, the whole universe. But when you are starting out with the training, if you start the meditation thinking about all beings without creating any specific focus, there is the possibility of the meditation becoming too general, intellectual, and vague. If that happens, your meditations will be beneficial, but they will not be that effective. Enjoying some idea or vague feeling of loving-kindness produces limited positive results, but a pure and strong experience of loving-kindness awakened from the depth of your heart eliminates your negative mental qualities and opens you, orienting your mind toward others with a force of boundless love.

We should start the meditation, then, by wishing joy for one person, someone who represents a powerful and inspiring image that will help us to invoke a spirited loving-kindness in our heart of hearts. Here, we start the meditation with our own mother—as Tibetan Buddhists always do. For many people, the mother represents a person of selfless love. But if you feel resistance toward this idea because you do not have an easy and loving relationship with your mother, use images of your father, or another family member such as a grandparent, or a very good friend, or a particularly helpful teacher—someone who has been a source of love in your life. If you love your mother, but you feel her love was not always perfect and unconditional, then contemplate that she had many challenges in her life and that she tried hard to be a good mother, even if she did not succeed in being perfect all the time.

We start with a person who evokes loving-kindness in us easily, without complications. We do not start with a person who brings up feelings of longing, attachment, lust, resentment, hatred, jealousy, or pain. After achieving a heartfelt wish for joy for that person, then we meditate for those who are neutral, then for those who trigger negative feelings, and then for many beings, and finally for all sentient beings. Je Tsongkhapa writes, "As the stages of meditation on loving-kindness: first meditate on friends and loved ones, then neutral ones, after that on foes, and finally focus on all beings."[9]

Meditate on the Source and the Object of Loving-Kindness

So visualize and bring to mind your mother, or the person who represents pure love for you, imagining that person in front of you in clear and vivid form. (I will refer to "your mother" in the instructions that follow, but substitute a person of uncomplicated loving-kindness in your life if your mother is not that person.)

With a relaxed mind, keep looking at her, or the person you choose, as the symbol of love. Keep enjoying her loving presence. Then look at her kind and beautiful face and see her eyes looking at you with undivided attention and unconditional love. Enjoy and celebrate her presence, her loving presence, her beautiful loving heart.

Then think, "Because of you, I am here on this earth. You are the person who gave me this amazing life." And, in the case of your mother, you could think, "You carried and cared for me for nine months in your womb. I am part of you and you welcomed me as part of your body. You cared for me at the expense of your own health, interests, or enjoyments. Ever since I was born, day and night, you never separated me from your loving thoughts. You sacrificed so many things in your life for my sake. You made me the apple of your eye. When I was sick, for days and nights, your sadness and fear for me stopped you from resting or sleeping. When I uttered my first words and took my first steps, your proud excitement had no limits and you kept repeating the news to all the neighbors, whoever would have the patience to listen. Your loving heart always thought of me first. Whenever I went out, your heart was always filled with worry for my safety. Your pure love always wished me to remain at your side. Whenever I left for school or work, half of your kind heart was always filled with joy for my future success but the other half was always filled with sadness from missing me or from fear of unknown things happening to me. Although at times you were in pain, you always showed me your cheerful face to encourage me and make me happier. All the happiness and success that I am enjoying is because of your unconditional love and dedication. From the depth of my heart, I am thankful and

grateful to you for your unconditional love and sacrifices."
Feel her presence and her love, returning to her image
again and again if your mind wanders.

Then think, "Like everyone else, my mother (or the
person you choose) always wishes to have happiness and a
meaningful life for herself and for all her loved ones. But
she has enjoyed very little true joy and lasting happiness.
She hates facing hardships for herself and her loved ones,
but she and her loved ones have endured disappointments,
sadness, old age, pain, and an unknown future."

Also think, "Now, before long, unfortunately, she has
to face the last days of her life and deal with the life after
death. According to Buddhism, a happy or unhappy life
after her death solely depends on positive or negative
mental habits that she has generated in her mind during
her lifetime. If she has enjoyed a mostly peaceful, joyful,
loving, caring, and respectful mind, then a happy future
will be assured for her. If she has harbored a great deal
of attachment, hatred, jealousy, and ignorance, then an
unpleasant future will be waiting for her. Now she has
spent all her time and energy taking care of her family
and loved ones and has never taken the opportunity to
improve the qualities and habits of her own life and mind
stream. So, the fate of her future is uncertain." Think care-
fully about her life and her unknown future.

Then say to yourself, "I have been blessed by the Buddha's loving-kindness and have awakened loving-kindness in myself. Now I will be able to pray for the loving-kindness of the Buddha for my mother and offer my own most precious loving-kindness to my beloved mother. How wonderful, and how lucky I am to enjoy such opportunities!" In your heart, feel the loving-kindness—that is, wishing joy for her from the depth of your heart. Remember that the thought and feeling of loving-kindness is the Buddha's blessing: the blessing of the Buddha of Loving-Kindness and blessings of the Buddha qualities of your own mind. Feel that your whole body and mind are blossoming with the blazing energy of loving-kindness. Rejoicing and celebrating the new dawn of the most precious mind of loving-kindness in your life, chant, OM MANI PADME HUNG.

Develop and Offer Your Own Loving-Kindness

Remember that your body has become a boundless body of blessing light—as if thousands of suns have risen in you. Your mind has transformed into the unconditional love of the Buddha filled with blissful heat, as you meditated in the earlier stages.

First, imagine that from your body of blessing light your unconditional love is emitted in the form of beams of radiant blazing light, and it reaches your mother. Those blessing beams of light of pure love are bright, colorful, and luminous. Those beams of light are filled with blissful heat and accompanied by celebratory sounds of OM MANI PADME HUNG (or AH). Slowly, your mother's body is fully and completely filled with the radiant rays and streams of luminous blessing light of loving-kindness, as if sunlight fills every part of the world around us. Feel the unity of your own unconditional love joined with the pure love of your mother, the symbol of love. Enjoy it and celebrate.

This love is not the love of attachment, grasping, craving, bias, or sensation, nor is it tainted with pain, but rather it is unconditional love of total openness, boundlessness, caring for others, joy, universal peace, and heartfelt celebration—in this love, you are totally wishing joy for your mother. Visualize and feel that all the sadness, fear, confusion, and pain of her life, along with the causes of these afflictions—the negative states of mind, the emotions, the habits, and their impact in the form of darkness in her body—are totally dispelled and have vanished by the power of the sunlight of your loving-kindness.

Feel, enjoy, and celebrate the great unity of your love and your mother's love as one. Enjoy that awareness of love. As you rejoice and celebrate the great unity of your love and your mother's love, chant, OM MANI PADME HUNG.

Purify and Transform the Object of Your Love through the Blessings of the Buddha

With your mind's eye, look at the Buddha of Loving-Kindness that you visualized earlier. Enjoy the amazingly beautiful presence of the Buddha and develop total devotion and trust in him. He is looking at and thinking of your mother with unconditional love, like a loving mother looking at her only child. Also imagine that your mother—who is sitting in front of you—is likewise looking at and seeing the Buddha with heartfelt devotion. She is joining you in the prayers and meditations.

Then chant the six-syllable prayer in the sweetest melody you can think of (loudly or in the mind's voice)—as the expression of your devotion to the Buddha. Imagine that your mother is joining you in the prayers, as you beseech the Buddha of Loving-Kindness to bestow the blessings of Buddha's unconditional love and omniscient wisdom upon your kind mother: OM MANI PADME HUNG.

Repeating the prayer with her, think that your mother's mind and heart are fully opening up and blossoming with joy, trust, and devotion—devotion to the Buddha, like a flower blossoming in the sunlight. Buddha's unconditional love has been invoked by the power of the prayer with devotion. As a result, from various parts of Buddha's body, multiple-colored beams of blessing light—light of unconditional love and omniscient wisdom of the Buddha with blissful heat—are emitted and reach your mother.

Slowly, her body is fully filled with the bright and colorful blessing light of unconditional love of the Buddha. All her negative states of mind—emotions, fear, sadness, pain, and confusion, along with their causes, the negative karmas, all in the form of darkness—are totally dispelled from her body. Her body—every particle, every corner of every particle, of her body—is fully filled with the blessing light of unconditional love, omniscient wisdom, and boundless power of the Buddha, filled with the energies of blissful heat and the pure sounds of AH. There is no trace of the darkness of sadness, fear, or pain left behind. Everything about her is filled with light, with the luminosity of loving-kindness of the Buddha.

Finally her body is totally transformed into a body of luminous blessing light. Her mind is fully transformed into a mind of loving-kindness and omniscient wisdom of the Buddha. Celebrating this great purification and transformation, chant, OM MANI PADME HUNG.

STAGE TEN—OFFERING LOVING-KINDNESS TO OTHERS AND TO ALL

If our meditation on loving-kindness has so far been based on openness and driven by the wish of joy for others, without falling into the traps of grasping and attachment, then in this stage we are ready to expand our loving-kindness to a neutral person, to a suffering person, to a so-called foe, to a group of beings, and finally to all beings as well as to the whole universe.

According to the teachings of Buddhism, this life is not the only one that we will have. Each of us has had infinite lives in the past, and therefore each being must have been our loving mother many times in the past. Each must have loved, cared for, and sacrificed her own life to make us happy, like our present mother. Furthermore, among this infinite number of beings, each and every one of them wants and has wanted to enjoy happiness and avoid hardships, but most beings indulge in negative deeds, the causes of suffering, instead of positive deeds, the causes of happiness. So the suffering of other beings is unlikely to end or ease.

With this in mind, recognize and celebrate that you have been blessed by the knowledge and experience of loving-kindness and the opportunity to share your loving-kindness with others. Celebrate your own good fortune of being in a position to help others.

Meditate on Loving-Kindness toward a Neutral Person

In this stage of the meditation, you should visualize a person toward whom you have no special feelings, positive or negative, and meditate on loving-kindness toward that person. With a relaxed mind, focus your loving mind's eyes on the person. Say to yourself, "This person must have been my loving mother a number of times in the past. Each time, this person must have given me my birth, cherished me as the most precious child in the world. This person must have sacrificed his or her own happiness for my happiness." Enjoy and celebrate the opportunity of having his or her loving presence in front of you. Then think, "Today, I am able to express gratitude to this person and repay him or her through the offerings of meditation on the Buddha and on loving-kindness. How fortunate am I!"

Remember that your body has been transformed into a body of blessed luminosity, a body of loving-kindness with blissful heat. Your mind has been blessed by the omniscient wisdom and loving-kindness of the Buddha.

Then visualize infinite, boundless particles of the blessing light of your body being emitted toward him or her—beams of blessing light of unconditional love with blissful heat and the celebratory sound of OM MANI PADME HUNG. The light of unconditional love totally fills his or her body. All the darkness in his or her body, the darkness that represents sadness, fear, confusion, pain, and negative karmas, has totally been dispelled. His or her body is completely filled with the blessing light of your unconditional love, filled with blissful heat.

As you offer loving-kindness toward this person, he or she becomes the object of the blessings of the Buddha of Loving-Kindness. The Buddha of Loving-Kindness sends out beams of blessing light of omniscient wisdom and unconditional love of the Buddha. The body of the person to whom you are offering loving-kindness is fully purified and transformed into a body of blessing light with blissful heat. His or her mind is transformed into a mind of unconditional love, a mind blessed with amazing peace, joy, and courage. Celebrating the great transformation, sing, OM MANI PADME HUNG.

Meditate on Loving-Kindness toward a Suffering Being

Next, visualize a person who is suffering mentally or physically, or visualize a person who has been involved in committing evil deeds that will bring a hellish future for him or her—and meditate on loving-kindness.

Again, remember that this person must have been your loving mother a number of times in the past. Each time, this person must have given you your birth and then cherished you as the most precious child in the world. He or she must have sacrificed his or her own happiness for your happiness. So, this person is a symbol of love for you, and you owe gratitude to him or her.

Now see that person visualized as a loving mother and see that he or she is suffering with sadness, fear, and pain.

Do not just think abstractly about the person's suffering, but feel in your heart what he or she might be feeling. Imagine for a moment if this person's suffering were never to be relieved. Recognize that there is no certainty of seeing any light of happiness in his or her life in the near future. With these possibilities in mind, develop your own strong wish and determination to release him or her from the pit of suffering and lead him or her to the light of happiness and joy through the power of loving-kindness and the Buddha.

Then remember that your body has been transformed into the body of blessing light of loving-kindness with blissful heat. Your mind has been blessed by the omniscient wisdom and loving-kindness of the Buddha. Develop a mind filled with joy, and celebrate by thinking, "I am blessed and empowered to gratefully repay this person for their kindness, through the offerings of meditation on the Buddha and on loving-kindness. How fortunate am I to have this opportunity. How wonderful it is!"

Then from your body of blessing light emit toward him or her beams of blessing light of unconditional love with blissful heat and the celebratory sound of OM MANI PADME HUNG (or AH). Those blessing beams of light of love totally fill his or her body. All the darkness in his or her body that represents sadness, fear, confusion, pain, and negative karmas is totally dispelled. Especially, the particular suffering that this person is enduring, with its karmic causes, is fully purified. His or her body and mind are fully filled with blessing light of unconditional love of the Buddha with blissful heat.

As you offer this meditation on loving-kindness toward a person who is suffering, the Buddha of Loving-Kindness sends beams of blessing light of omniscient wisdom and unconditional love. The body of that person is fully purified and transformed into a body of blessing light with blissful heat. His or her mind is transformed into a mind of omniscient wisdom and unconditional love of the Buddha, a mind filled with amazing peace, joy, and courage. Celebrate the great transformation by singing, OM MANI PADME HUNG.

Meditate on Loving-Kindness toward a So-Called Foe

In this part of the meditation, visualize a person whom you view as an enemy and meditate on loving-kindness.

Think that he or she must have been your loving mother a number of times in the past. Each time, he or she must have given you your birth and then cherished you as the most precious child in the world. This person must have sacrificed his or her happiness for your happiness. Understand that he or she is therefore a person of love for you, and you owe gratitude to him or her.

If this person whom you consider a foe has been cruel

to you, you could try to be even more compassionate and caring to him or her. Imagine, for example, if you saw someone badly injured in a road accident: you would do your best to ease that person's pain. You could likewise view your enemy as a person who is injured, but in this case the injury is emotional and spiritual. According to Buddhist teaching, if a person is cruel and harmful to someone, then as the consequences of that action, the person will suffer with intolerable afflictions in his or her future lives. If a person has been cruel to you, therefore, he or she will suffer in future lives. With this in mind, you can understand the need to be even more loving and caring for this person. If you tolerate his or her cruelty and meditate on loving-kindness in return, the merit of developing such patience and loving-kindness will be even greater than the merit of having loving-kindness for a gentle person. Thus, your so-called foe is giving you the great gift of a golden opportunity to gain merit, which is something to be thankful for.

Visualize, then, and imagine that from your body beams of blessing light of unconditional love with blissful heat and the celebratory sound of OM MANI PADME HUNG (or AH) go out toward the person as an offering. That light of unconditional love totally fills his or her body. All the darkness in his or her body that represents sadness, fear, confusion, pain, and negative karmas is totally dispelled and purified. Most important, the karmic causation of the cruel deeds that he or she has been committing is fully purified without leaving even a trace. His or her body and mind are filled with the blessing light of unconditional love with blissful heat. He or she has transformed into a person of peace, love, and joy, with blossoming smiles.

Through your meditation, the Buddha of Loving-Kindness sends beams of blessing light of wisdom and love toward the person you saw as your enemy. That person's body is fully purified and transformed into a body of blessing light with blissful heat. His or her mind is transformed into a mind of omniscient wisdom and unconditional love of the Buddha, a mind of amazing peace and joy. Celebrate the great transformation by singing, OM MANI PADME HUNG.

Meditate on Loving-Kindness toward a Group of People

In the next step, direct your meditation on loving-kindness toward a group of people or animals that you know.

Again remember that all these beings must have been your loving mothers a number of times in the past. Each time, they must have given you your birth and then cherished you as the most precious child in the world. They must have sacrificed their happiness for your happiness. They are symbols of love for you, and you owe them gratitude.

Then visualize and think that your blessing-light body emits toward them beams of light of omniscient wisdom and unconditional love with blissful heat and the celebratory sound of OM MANI PADME HUNG (or AH). The light of unconditional love totally fills their bodies. All the darkness in their bodies and minds that represents sadness, fear, confusion, pain, and negative karmas is totally dispelled and purified. Their bodies are completely filled with the blessing light of unconditional love with blissful heat.

Through your meditation, the Buddha of Loving-Kindness sends them his blessing beams of light of wisdom and unconditional love. Their bodies are fully purified and transformed into bodies of blessing light with blissful heat. Their minds are purified and transformed into minds of omniscient wisdom and unconditional love of the Buddha, minds of amazing peace and joy. Celebrate this great transformation by singing, OM MANI PADME HUNG.

Meditate on Loving-Kindness toward All Beings and the Whole Universe

Now, meditate on loving-kindness toward all: human beings, animals, visible beings, invisible beings, the beings of all the six realms and the whole universe.

Remember that each and every being must have been your loving mother a number of times in the past. Every time, they must have given you your birth, then cherished you as their dearest and most precious child in the world. They must have sacrificed their happiness for your happiness. So they are all symbols of love for you, and you owe them gratitude.

Your body of blessing light emits beams of blessing light of wisdom and unconditional love with blissful heat and the celebratory sound of OM MANI PADME HUNG (or AH) in all directions, as offerings to all. The blessing light of unconditional love totally fills the bodies of every being and the whole universe. All the darkness in their bodies and the universe that represents sadness, fear, confusion, suffering, and negative karmas is totally dispelled. Their bodies and the whole universe are totally filled with luminous blessing light with blissful heat. Their minds are filled with the blessing light of unconditional love.

Through your meditation, the Buddha of Loving-Kindness sends blessing light of omniscient wisdom and unconditional love in all directions. The body of every being is fully filled with this light, purified of all the darkness of suffering and negative karmas, which are dispelled without leaving any trace. The bodies of all beings are transformed into bodies of blessing light with blissful heat. Their minds are transformed into minds of omniscient wisdom and unconditional love of the Buddha, filled with boundless peace and joy. The whole universe is purified, healed, and transformed into a universe of pure light, a light of peace, joy, and loving-kindness.

Feel the unconditional love, the loving openness, pervading all beings and uniting all as the light of love. There is no individual ego to hold, cherish, or preserve. All are one in the awareness of the light of boundless love. Seeing and feeling thus—celebrate this great transformation and unity by singing, OM MANI PADME HUNG.

Meditation for Fulfilling
Individual Wishes

Now meditate on and pray to the Buddha of Loving-Kindness for fulfilling any particular wish or reaching any specific positive goal for yourself or others, whatever that may be.

Some people may think that praying for your own health or for some other benefit to yourself, rather than praying strictly for the benefit of others, is a selfish form of meditation or that it is not proper. But there is nothing wrong with praying and meditating to improve your own health or other elements of your life. Such meditation is positive. If you meditate for your health because being healthier makes you a better resource for serving others, for example, then your efforts can be viewed as part of the training undertaken by seekers of enlightenment (in Sanskrit, *bodhisattva*)—your meditation becomes an ideal practice, because of the positive qualities of your mental attitude and because of your purpose, the positive goal.

Even if your meditations and prayers have been initiated with the intention of fulfilling your own needs, such as your health, meditation on loving-kindness and the Buddha of Loving-Kindness by its very nature cannot remain selfish because it will turn into a source of benefits for many. The amazing beauty of meditation on loving-kindness is that it fundamentally transforms your mind and whole being and approach, placing them onto a path of perfection. No darkness of negative emotions will survive in the light of meditation on loving-kindness. Emotional burning will end, as the fire of negative thoughts and karmas is extinguished in the depth of the great sea of loving-kindness. Meditation on loving-kindness spontaneously pacifies all your mental, emotional, physical, and karmic dilemmas and transforms your life into a life filled with peace, joy, and benefits for yourself as well as for others.

The following are some of the ways of applying meditations on loving-kindness to your day-to-day life:

First, refresh the presence of the Buddha of Loving-Kindness in your mind. His majestic body is luminous and made of immaculate light. His mind is the mind of omniscient wisdom, unconditional love, and boundless power. Feel his vivid presence, the majestic body of loving-kindness.

Next, pray to the Buddha from the depth and totality of your mind and with complete openness of your heart. Transform the energy waves and sound waves of your body and the whole universe into the energy waves of joy and devotional prayers, by singing, OM MANI PADME HUNG. See and feel that your mind, heart, body, and every particle of your body are opening, blossoming, and shining with energy waves of devotion and trust in the Buddha. Devote the six-syllable prayer to the goal of pacifying your emotions or accomplishing some other particular objective, if you have one.

Then, receive omniscient wisdom and unconditional love of the Buddha in the form of beams of blessing-light nectar with blissful heat and with the celebratory sound of OM MANI PADME HUNG (or AH). Your body is fully filled with the blessing light. The darkness in your body that represents your problems (whatever they are) is totally dispelled and purified, without leaving any trace behind.

Finally, your body is totally transformed into the body of blessing light of unconditional love of the Buddha. Celebrating the great transformation, sing, OM MANI PADME HUNG.

In addition to the meditations above, you could also add any of the following meditations and prayers to your daily practice to accomplish any particular wish for your life that belongs to one of "the four means of action": the actions of pacifying, increasing, dominating, and destroying. These four means of action relate to specific meditation practices. Meditation on loving-kindness can fulfill any of the four actions. As a meditation on peace, it pacifies and heals all problems. As a meditation on development, it increases prosperity. As a meditation on power, it helps us to gain control over all circumstances. And as a meditation on wrathful actions, it eliminates all negative forces. As the master Paltrul Rinpoche wrote,

> As the concepts of two obscurations are pacified,
>   the experiences and realizations will be increased.
> As you enjoy control over your mind, all the foes
>   will be subjugated.
> It is Avalokiteshvara who grants the common
>   and uncommon accomplishments in this very
>   lifetime.
> Recite the six-syllables as the accomplishment of
>   the four actions.
>
> Subdue your enemy—hatred—with the weapon of
>   loving-kindness.
> Serve your family, the beings of the six realms, with
>   skillful means of compassion.
> In the fertile field of devotion, cultivate the crop
>   of meditative experiences and realizations.
> Recite the six-syllables as the completion of this
>   life's work.[10]

Additional Meditations—
The Four Actions

You can use the meditation on loving-kindness as the source and means of exercises of the "four actions," what Paltrul Rinpoche calls the "common accomplishments." If your heart is saturated with loving-kindness, whatever you do, for yourself or others—all will become the expression of loving-kindness in one of the four actions.

Loving-kindness is the indispensable foundation, the essence and means, to practice the following four actions. Without loving-kindness, your efforts in these "common accomplishments" could instead become the foundation and enforcement of rigid thought, selfish motivations, greedy passions, and distracting emotions, which will cause only pain and confusion.

The Peaceful Action

Meditation, ceremony, or any activity that pacifies the negative aspects of a person or of the world is a "peaceful action."

Visualize and feel that the white light of love of the Buddha of Loving-Kindness has come, filling and transforming your body into a body of light, the light of loving-kindness. In this way, all the mental and physical problems suffered by yourself or others have been pacified, purified, and healed. Your body and mind have been transformed into the light of peace, joy, and loving-kindness of the Buddha. Because of this transformation, every action of your life will now be an enlightening "action of peace." Enjoying such meditation, sing, OM MANI PADME HUNG.

See and feel that the dark clouds of sadness and fear that shade your life are dispelled without leaving any trace behind—they are lifted by the power of the blazing light of the Buddha of Loving-Kindness. Your body has been filled with and transformed into a body of light as if thousands of suns of boundless love have arisen in you. As you enjoy this transformation in your body, your mind is feeling it and being transformed as well. When your mind and body are transformed into the light of the Buddha of Loving-Kindness, all your surroundings will be transformed, and the world will become a world of light of love. Enjoying such meditation, sing, OM MANI PADME HUNG.

See and feel that the burning flames of sickness and pain within your body, mind, or heart are healed by the nectar stream of light of the Buddha of Loving-Kindness. Acknowledge and appreciate this freedom from pain, and enjoy the healthy feeling of peace and joy that is created by the light of loving-kindness. Enjoying such meditation, sing, OM MANI PADME HUNG.

See and feel that all the stress created by the tightness of dualistic concepts, by cravings for what you want and hate, by fear of dangers and failures, by hopes for esteem, fame, and material gains is released and eased through the power of the blessing light of the Buddha of Loving-Kindness. Your body has become a body of light, and not a trace remains of mental and emotional stress. Your mind has become a mind of loving-kindness, and all the thoughts and feelings within your mind have transformed into a unified feeling of being totally awake, open, and radiant. Enjoying such meditation, sing, OM MANI PADME HUNG.

See and feel that all the filth of the afflicting emotions within your mind—hatred, greed, jealousy, arrogance, and confusions with their causes—is washed away and purified by the blessing stream of nectar of the Buddha of Loving-Kindness. Your clean body is filled with the blessing-light nectar of loving-kindness, omniscient wisdom, and the boundless power of Buddha. Enjoying such meditation, sing, OM MANI PADME HUNG.

Easing a relationship problem: Visualize your boss, employee, or any person with whom you are having an interpersonal problem. Pray to the Buddha, bringing a stream of blessing light of love from the Buddha of Loving-Kindness. Imagining the person with whom you are experiencing a difficult relationship, fill his or her body with the light of love with blissful heat. See and feel that his or her body has transformed into a body of blessing light. His or her stress, worries, and unhealthy habits, in the form of burning flames, are extinguished by the nectar stream of light. His or her mind is transformed into a mind of peace, joy, and love, total love. His or her face is blossoming with a smile of joy. Experience his or her feeling of loving-kindness in your heart and unite with it as one joy of loving-kindness. Enjoying such meditation, sing, OM MANI PADME HUNG.

Such meditation pacifies the person's mind and at the same time, especially, it pacifies your own mental attitude and perception of that person.

Healing sickness: Visualize and feel that from the Buddha of Loving-Kindness a warm stream of nectar-of-light with herbal medicinal taste and blissful heat has flooded down. From the top of your head, it has gradually filled your body and every particle of your body. All the sicknesses, impurities, toxicities, and sick cells within your body, with their karmic causes and emotional conditions, are washed away. All your physical and mental ills caused by imbalances and injuries are fully cleansed. There is no trace of illness left in your body. Then your body is filled and filled fully with the blessing nectar of boundless bliss and loving-kindness. Finally, see and enjoy that your body has transformed into a blessing-light body of great health, strength, vigor, and radiance, and your mind has transformed into a mind of great joy and unconditional love of

the Buddha. Enjoying such meditation, sing, OM MANI
PADME HUNG.

If you are performing healing meditation for another
person, meditate that both you and the person (or
all beings) are praying, and that he or she is receiving
blessings and being healed, instead of just you.

To help the dying or dead: Offer the following meditations and prayers for those who are about to die, who
are dying, who have been dead for some time, or who
might now be taking rebirth.

Imagine and feel that both you and the person—in
his or her living form as you know (or knew) them—
are sitting calmly and looking at the Buddha of Loving-
Kindness in the sky in front of you. Buddha is looking at
you with his clear eyes, directly, with unconditional love.
You both are seeing the amazing images of Buddha and
the ocean of Enlightened Ones who are with him. Buddha is the embodiment of all the Enlightened Ones and
the representation of the pure qualities of the whole universe. He is the reflection of your own enlightened qualities. You and the person you are thinking of are enjoying
together the warmth, unconditional love, omniscient wisdom, and boundless power of the Buddha. And to what-

ever degree you yourself are enjoying the meditation and blessings, to that same degree the meditation will enable you to help others more effectively.

Vocally or mentally, sing the six-syllable prayer repeatedly, with energy of devotion and confidence in the Buddha from the depth and totality of your heart: OM MANI PADME HUNG. Visualize the other person doing the same.

Then visualize and feel that from the Buddha streams of blessing light—the light of unconditional love of the Buddha with blissful heat—have come and completely filled your and the other person's body. Enjoy it again and again.

All your negative karmas, negative states of mind, and afflicting emotions—fear, sadness, pain, and confusion—all your and the other person's physical and mental ills, present in the form of darkness, are totally purified and dispelled by the blazing light of the Buddha.

Your bodies are transformed into pure bodies of blessing light of the Buddha. The whole atmosphere is filled with Buddha blessing, with peace and joy. Your minds are transformed into minds of loving-kindness of the Buddha. Enjoying such meditation, sing, OM MANI PADME HUNG.

Then, if you like, you can add the following meditations to help the dying or the dead: Visualize and believe that the person you have in mind is following the Buddha of Loving-Kindness—with great joy and confidence—along with an ocean of Enlightened Ones in various forms, colors, and costumes. They all have flown away toward the Blissful Pure Land (a paradise of the Buddhas that is free from pain and sorrow), in the western direction, through the path of beams of rainbow-like light in the sky, with an amazing display of celebrations of music and prayers.

They all have landed in the amazingly beautiful and joyful Blissful Pure Land. The person of whom you are thinking has miraculously taken instant rebirth in a giant lotus in the Blissful Pure Land.[11] The Blissful Pure Land is the pure land of the Buddha of Infinite Light (Amitabha) as well as of the Buddha (or bodhisattva) of Loving-Kindness. The person of whom you are thinking is enjoying the sublime beauty and joy of the pure land. He or she is seeing and enjoying the presence and blessings of the Buddha of Infinite Light and the Buddha of Loving-Kindness, who is manifesting there as the bodhisattva of loving-kindness.

With great joy and confidence, proclaim and celebrate that person's freedom from the suffering of samsara and his or her rebirth in the Blissful Pure Land, filled with the awareness of ultimate peace and joy. Celebrating the great rebirth, sing, OM MANI PADME HUNG.

The Action of Increasing

Meditation, ceremony, or any other activity that increases prosperity—quality of life, health, wealth, happiness, meditation skill, level of spiritual realization—whether benefiting oneself or others, is an "action of increasing."

Visualize and feel that the power of the yellow light of loving-kindness of the Buddha has filled and transformed your body (or the body of someone else) into a body of blessing light, light of loving-kindness. All your qualities, life, and prosperity are expanded, developed, made to blossom, and strengthened with no limit. With this transformation, every action of your life is also transformed, into an enlightening "action of increasing." Enjoying such meditation, sing, OM MANI PADME HUNG. The following meditations also serve as actions of increasing that you might use if they suit your need.

See and feel that all the aspects of your life such as virtues, merit, wisdom, and things you enjoy (any or all of these) are increased, strengthened, opened, and made to blossom limitlessly by the force of the blazing light of loving-kindness of the Buddha, just as flowers blossom in the sunlight. Enjoying such meditation, sing, OM MANI PADME HUNG.

See and feel that your spiritual and meditative experiences and realizations are increased, clarified, refined, and perfected by the light of wisdom and of loving-kindness

of the Buddha. Enjoying such meditation, sing, OM MANI
PADME HUNG.

You can apply the meditation on loving-kindness as an
action of increasing—for improving your mental or physical life or your material prosperity—in the following ways,
if you wish:

For longevity: See and feel that the power of the infinite
beams of light of loving-kindness has brought the blessings of longevity in the form of rich blazing white light
and life-force energies from infinite Buddhas and from
various sources—sages, people, sacred objects, mountains, fields, trees, flowers, fruits, lakes, rivers, ocean, and
sky. These bright white beams of the light of longevity
have filled your body, every particle of your body. You
have received the power of longevity and your body is
fully transformed into a body of light of longevity. All the
decay of your life force is fully restored. Imagine and feel
that your attainment of longevity has been consecrated,
confirmed, stabilized, and secured in you by the power of
the loving-kindness of the Buddha. Enjoying such meditation, sing, OM MANI PADME HUNG.

For prosperity: See and feel that the power of the infinite
beams of colorful light of loving-kindness has brought
all the blessings of prosperity—of spiritual attainments,

wealth, offspring, knowledge, wisdom, and power. Your life is filled with the prosperity of peace, joy, and confidence; your body is filled with health, vigor, and youthfulness; your house is filled with people, treasures, joy, and laughter; your surroundings are filled with peace, beauty, harmony, enjoyments, and celebrations. Feel the fullness and richness of your life.

As you complete this meditation, recognize and feel that by the power of the light of loving-kindness, the glorious activities and services of your prosperous life are fulfilling the needs of all—whomever you see, hear, or touch. Your experience of loving-kindness has increased and is blossoming with no limit. Celebrating the great attainments of increase, sing, OM MANI PADME HUNG.

The Action of Power

Meditation, ceremony, or any other activity directed toward gaining or maintaining power over oneself or over other beings or material forces, for the benefit of oneself or others, is an "action of power."

Visualize and feel that the power of the red light of loving-kindness has filled and transformed your body, or the body of someone else, into a body of red-colored blessing light, the light of loving-kindness. Beams of lights of your body have gathered up and brought to you all the blessings and prosperity of existence, and these have merged into you. You now enjoy control over your own mind and emotions through the boundless and overwhelming power of the light of loving-kindness. Most important, the strength of your trust and confidence in loving-kindness is magnified and maximized.

Enjoy the absolute control over your own mind and emotions through the overwhelming power of the light of loving-kindness. If you have control over your own mind, then your egoless open mind will enjoy power over all that you encounter with limitless energy. Not only do you have control over your own mind, emotions, and life, but you can also influence the minds and lives of many. In this way, you can serve others and transform the lives of many into lives that are saturated with the light of loving-kindness of the Buddha. Every action of your life is now transformed into an enlightening "action of power." Celebrating the great power, sing, OM MANI PADME HUNG.

The Wrathful Action

Meditation, ceremony, or any other activity that eliminates a harmful influence or situation through the powerful force of loving-kindness is a "wrathful action."

Visualize and feel that the invincible power of the light of loving-kindness has filled, overwhelmed, and transformed your body into a body of light of loving-kindness, the invincible power. Enjoy the anger-free wrathful action of loving-kindness that subdues and eliminates all harsh and rigid negative forces, with the ultimate force of ultimate love.

See and feel that the tight, rigid, and concrete ego of yourself and others, your intense mental concepts, afflicting emotions, destructive actions, harmful karmic forces, and warring forces, as well as brutal epidemics and natural calamities that are hard to pacify through peaceful actions, must be subjugated and conquered by the overwhelming wrathful action of the light of loving-kindness. All harmful things are transformed into the light of loving-kindness of the Buddha, by your body of light of loving-kindness, the invincible power. Every action of your life is now transformed into an enlightening "action of wrath," the invincible force of loving-kindness. Celebrating the ultimate victory, sing, OM MANI PADME HUNG.

The Uncommon Attainments

Meditation, ceremony, or any other activity that leads you to ultimate peace, joy, and omniscience—to Buddhahood—are the ways to uncommon attainment, the "uncommon accomplishments" addressed along with the four actions in the verse by Paltrul Rinpoche above.

See and feel that infinite beams of blessing light of loving-kindness with blissful heat have come from the Buddha and filled your body, every particle of your body.

All negative states of mind, emotions, and karmic causations rooted in grasping at mental objects in the form of darkness are totally purified by the brightness of the Buddha's blessing light of wisdom and love.

Your body is transformed into the body of blessing light. Your mind is transformed into a mind of omniscient wisdom, unconditional love, and boundless power of the Buddha. Your mind has become inseparable from Buddha's wisdom, love, and power. Generosity, moral discipline, tolerance, diligence, tranquility, and wisdom—the six perfections—are developed and fully perfected in you. Your heart is filled with the energy of boundless love, compassion, joy, evenness, fearlessness, courage, confidence, and openness. Develop confidence that you have attained "the uncommon accomplishments," the nature and pure qualities of Buddhahood.

Believe that absolute awareness of wisdom, love, and power—the qualities of the true nature of your mind—has awakened and been perfected in you. Remain in the awareness of the loving-kindness of the Buddha and the loving-kindness of your own mind in union—without grasping at this unity or conceptualizing it. As an expression of the power of the awareness of such union, sing, OM MANI PADME HUNG.

According to the teachings of Buddhism, the number of beings is immeasurable and the number of world systems is infinite. From that perspective, if you develop loving-kindness toward all the immeasurable beings and develop the wish of fulfilling all the immeasurable needs of every being in every world, then such an attitude itself becomes immeasurable. Then, as the result, you will generate immeasurable merit and wisdom together with enjoying immeasurable benefits. Shantideva, an eighth-century Buddhist scholar, wrote:

> If the thought of benefiting one person
> Is superior to making offerings to the Buddha,
> Then [the merit of] making the effort
> To serve all beings must be worthwhile.[12]

STAGE ELEVEN—
CONTEMPLATE THE AWARENESS OF
THE MEDITATION RESULT

With calm and relaxed mind, see if you are experiencing an awareness of loving-kindness or any other kinds of positive feelings, such as peace, joy, openness, and spaciousness, that have been generated in you as the result of the meditation. If you are enjoying any particular positive experience, first, recognize it. Then appreciate and celebrate the dawn of such fruition.

Then rest in the awareness of loving-kindness, as if you

have become one with it. Awareness means, at this stage, that you are totally awakened and alert; you are realizing and experiencing the result but without any (or with very little) grasping, clinging, attachment, or sensation. If you pour water into another vessel of water, both will become one body of water. In the same way, let the subject, your mind, and the object, the feeling of loving-kindness, become one—experience the awareness of loving-kindness as an ultimate peace that is totally open and boundless. Yes, meditation on loving-kindness starts with dualistic concepts and feelings associated with the senses, but it should lead to the goal of gaining vivid awareness of all in a state of oneness. Rest and rest endlessly in that awareness state of loving-kindness, without grasping at it or conceptualizing it; come back to it again and again.

Such meditation in awareness will bring the power of the meditation result into a deeper level of your mind, so that it will become more effective. Treasuring the fruit of your meditation at this deeper state, in the calm and peaceful sphere of your mind, will also make the meditation result longer lasting. This technique of contemplation in awareness can also be practiced as one of the higher states of meditation and realization, or it could lead you to one of these states.

Regarding higher states of meditation, however, we might address here the circumstance of meditators who say, "I am not interested in meditating on loving-kindness or devotion, because they are too conceptual and emotional. I want to transcend mental and emotional afflictions by meditating on emptiness, the nature of the mind, or the Buddha-nature."

The fact is that although realization of emptiness or Buddha-nature is the ultimate goal of almost all the Mahayana approaches, in order to reach that goal you must prepare yourself by training in the steps that will lead you there. And you must start your journey from where you are standing. Some meditators think, "I have studied the highest teachings from the best masters, and I have been studying for decades. So I am now qualified to focus only on the highest meditation." But although it is wonderful to have great teachers, and to study the highest teachings for a long time, you yourself can only come to the realization of Buddha-nature by authentic experience; the teachings will not perform this magic for you. Ambitions and boasting about your level of attainment might be thought of as high mountains of arrogance that can blind you to your path and that you need to overcome. A proverb says, "Having perfect teaching is not enough. The person must be perfect."

Many meditators arrive at a so-called emptiness state that is merely a state contrived by mind. Staying in meditation by grasping and clinging to the cozy feelings of the mind is not the same as meditation on emptiness or pure contemplation. The Tibetan saint Milarepa warned,

> The primordial emptiness that is arisen in the mind
> And the absence-of-thoughts that is contrived by
> the mind
> Have similarities, so, be careful not to mistake one
> for the other.
> Securing the innate nature through meditation
> And clinging to the taste of contemplation
> Have similarities, so, be careful not to mistake one
> for the other.[13]

A state in which you experience mere absence of any active thoughts is a state that lacks wisdom of awareness. Such a state is not a way of waking up from confusion, but rather it is a form of falling backward into confusion, a form of unconsciousness or spacing out. When meditators mistakenly believe that the neutral state they are anchoring in is a higher attainment than meditations such as those on loving-kindness and devotion, they are entertaining ideas that strengthen their ego, inflame their arrogance, and ultimately drive them to be contemptuous of others. The karma of such habitual mental tendencies will cause rebirth only in the animal realm or the formless realm at best.

Another thing to understand is that in such a neutral

state, you will essentially be grasping at some mental objects, sensations at a subtle level. In this state, therefore, you will not be achieving any liberation, but rather you will be trapping yourself further in the inner confinement caused by the usual habits of grasping and attachment.

Many people feel burned out and exhausted from bearing the heavy weight of emotional, physical, and social obligations—day in and day out. They seek a way to escape. The prospect of arriving at some sort of empty feeling where they can crawl in for a while sounds attractive to them. But such an escape is partial, temporary, and unworthy, and it should not be the path and goal of your precious life.

By contrast, the right meditations such as meditation on loving-kindness and contemplation in awareness will certainly lead to the realization of true emptiness (or openness), the nature of the mind, omniscient Buddhahood. In order to reach that goal, however, you must choose the right path—which means the path that suits you but not necessarily the path you like. In order to find the right path, you must first determine the nature of your own mental qualities, deciding whether they are mainly negative, positive, or perfect.

Negative: This is a mental state mainly occupied by negative thoughts, feelings, and emotions—such as hatred and anger, attachment and greed, jealousy and arrogance, confusion and misunderstanding—all rooted in grasping tightly at mental objects. In this state, the wheel of your life keeps turning from negative to negative, and as a consequence you repeatedly experience pain, sadness, fear, and confusion, as well as rebirths in unhappy realms. Whatever you do, your actions will also harm others. Unfortunately, most of us belong to this category.

Positive: This is a mental state mainly occupied by positive thoughts, feelings, and emotions—such as loving-kindness and compassion, peace and calm, respect and devotion, positive attitudes and perceptions, openness and feeling at ease. In this state, your mind is still dualistic, grasping, and emotional, but it is more open and at ease than the negative mind. Your life will be a life of a positive cycle. As the result, you will enjoy peace, joy, confidence, and happiness, as well as rebirths in joyful realms and pure lands (paradises of total peace and joy). Whatever you do, your actions will help others. The lives of some gifted people belong to this category.

Perfection: If you have realized the true nature of your mind and perfected that realization, then your mind will be free from dualistic concepts and emotions. Perfection of the true nature of your mind, of innate awareness, is the utmost peaceful and joyful state—as it is free from grasping, conflicts, afflictions, sensations, pain, or confusion. It is luminous omniscience and openness, like the union of sunlight and boundless space. Realization and perfection of the absolute nature of the mind is the attainment of Buddhahood. Very few people enjoy such perfections.

So, if your mind is occupied mostly by negative emotions, first, you must focus on purifying them and getting freedom from them through positive approaches such as devotion, pure perception, and serving others. When your mind functions mainly with positive thoughts and feelings, then and only then you should start to train on the path of perfection, the ultimate goal.

As long as your mind is occupied with negative ideas and emotions, even if your ultimate goal is perfection, you cannot jump from negative mind to perfection. Even if you have devoted yourself to the best teachings, your jumping effort might only land you in the ditch of the neutral state with no awakening or enlightenment, because your mind is not yet prepared for such a goal. Only when your mind is purified and refined by positive training will the realization of perfection become feasible.

Therefore, if you have already refined your mind with training on the positive path and are ready to start on the path of perfection, then this eleventh stage is the meditation on the union of awareness and emptiness (openness), the true nature of your mind. If you are not yet ready for the path of perfection, this stage is for bringing the results of your meditation on loving-kindness into a deeper level of your mind, as discussed before. So, remaining in such awareness, sing, OM MANI PADME HUNG. And contemplate the words of Paltrul Rinpoche:

Your mind is the union of awareness and emptiness, the *dharmakaya* [the ultimate body],
Rest in its innate state, without modification. The self-luminosity will arise.
Complete all that is to be done by just stopping all and doing nothing.
Recite the six syllables by dwelling in the naked union of awareness and emptiness.

Realizing all phenomena as emptiness is the crucial point of view.
It liberates all the concepts of truth and falsehood into their true nature.
Unite—without clinging—all the existents of samsara and nirvana as the *dharmakaya*,
Recite the six syllables as the self-liberation of all thoughts.

Clinging to the appearances as real is delusion, the cause of samsara.

Mind remaining in its natural state, free from
thoughts, is Avalokiteshvara.

Resting in Natural Mind is not other than [being in]
Avalokiteshvara.

Recite the six syllables by remaining in the nature of
the mind, the *dharmakaya*.[14]

Stage Twelve— Dedicate the Merit to Others and Make Aspirations

At the end of the meditation session dedicate all the merit
or positive karma, the deeds of the meditation and prayers,
to others—to your mother, to a neutral person, to a so-
called foe, and to all beings as the cause of happiness, peace,
and the realization of awareness of loving-kindness. Feel
happiness for having this merit and giving it away to bring
benefit to others.

If you dedicate the merit of loving-kindness to others or offer any positive deeds toward others with loving-
kindness, you will generate merit, positive karma,
bringing future happiness for yourself. If you give away
your merit, it will not actually be lost or decrease—it will
increase, because giving the gift of merit to others is itself
an important and powerful means of merit-making.

Now that the merit has been dedicated, invoke the

power of the Enlightened Ones and make positive aspirations. Think and say, "By the power of the Buddha of Loving-Kindness, and by the power of the merit of my prayers and meditations on loving-kindness, may all beings, without exception, receive and be inseparable from the blessing light of omniscient wisdom and unconditional love of the Buddha of Loving-Kindness. May the darkness of mental and emotional afflictions, fears and sadness, mental and physical ills, and confusion and struggles of the whole universe be pacified by the power of the blessing light of the Buddha's loving-kindness. May every being realize the blessing light, omniscient wisdom, and unconditional love of the Buddha and remain inseparable from them.

"May I always remain in union with the luminous blessing light, and the omniscient wisdom, and the unconditional love of the Buddha. May I be the source of the Buddha's blessings for all beings and especially for those who are close to me, are connected with me, and rely on me."

Benefits of the Twelve Stages of Meditation

Physically, these meditations are helpful in easing tension, by balancing the elements of earth, water, fire, and air, the building blocks of the body. They will clear and open the blocked veins, arteries, and channels of the body.

They will reconnect different organs, limbs, and parts of the body to allow them to work together in unity as one body. They will nourish the sick and dying particles of the body, bringing these particles back into life through the power of blessing light, blessing energies, and unconditional love.

Mentally, through the power of the light of loving-kindness of the Buddha, you are likely to feel that the tightness of the grip within your mind as it grasps at mental objects has been loosened; the meditations can purify the afflicting emotions and ease your sadness, fear, confusion, and pain.

As soon as your mind is transformed into the mind of loving-kindness, all the expressions of your body will become expressions of love and peace. You may become the very presence of loving-kindness of the Buddha for others. Or at least, you will become a person who is joyful and easy to be with.

Remember again the cycle: that when you see, hear, and feel the images, sounds, and feelings of loving-kindness, your mind is transformed into the mind of loving-kindness. When your mind becomes the mind of loving-kindness, whatever you see, hear, or feel will become images, sounds, and feelings of loving-kindness. Your life will become a blessed life, a cycle of loving-kindness.

Finally, at the time of your death, your mind will

become free from the constraints of the physical body, environmental energies, and social bondage. So if you have trained on loving-kindness and have contemplated devotion to the Buddha of Loving-Kindness, then you will move with great ease through the path of rainbow-like light and reach the Blissful Pure Land, a world of everlasting peace and joy, to take rebirth there.

Ordinary people with dualistic minds and emotional conflicts will experience the Blissful Pure Land as a place that is distant from them. However, highly accomplished meditators will find the Blissful Pure Land, the world or atmosphere of ultimate peace and joy, in themselves and around them at the time of their death as well as while they are alive. For them, the Blissful Pure Land arises instantly, right where they are because their merit has been perfected and their wisdom eyes have opened. There is no need of transporting themselves into another place, as taking rebirth there is simply a change of perception and conditions.

Infinite manifestations of the Buddha of Loving-Kindness appear in various forms at different places, such as at Mount Potala, but his main manifested pure land and the principle source of his manifestations is the Blissful Pure Land.[15] Once you are born in the Blissful Pure Land, you will be able to see infinite beings of the ordinary world with your clairvoyance and you will be able to serve them with boundless power and unconditional love, provided that they are receptive to your kindness and blessings.

According to Buddhism, the happiness of your future rebirths is totally dependent upon the nature of your past deeds—what you are doing now. So if you have trained your mind in loving-kindness, then for the time being your life will be peaceful and joyful, and ultimately it will lead you to enlightenment, the attainment of Buddhahood.

Yes, as long as you are on the path of training, your experience of loving-kindness will be dualistic, based in the senses, and emotional—but your meditation will also have meritorious and beneficial qualities. And when you reach the goal of training, Buddhahood, your loving-kindness will no longer be dualistic, based in the senses, or emotional: it will become the perfection of wisdom that spontaneously sees all and serves all, all the time. The great teacher Mipham Namgyal wrote, "When you perfect and transform all into the sublime wisdom of Buddhahood, the result, you will have no ordinary mind and mental events . . . With great compassion (or loving-kindness), you see and care for all infinite beings, all the time—throughout the six watches of the days and nights—and provide them with happiness and benefit."[16]

Incorporating Twelve-Stage Meditation into Everyday Life

To establish a firm footing at the beginning of your practice, it is essential to start by spending a few days fully devoted to meditating on the twelve-stage training. After that, each day you should meditate for a few hours. After establishing some solid experience in the meditation, you could condense the twelve-stage meditation into a shorter format that will fulfill your needs and suit your time, and practice that as your daily meditation. Start your condensed meditation with stage two. Then focus mainly on stages four, five, six, and seven. After that, offer your loving-kindness to "all" as given in stage ten. Then contemplate as taught in stage eleven as you like, and conclude with a brief dedication and aspiration as taught in stage twelve. After establishing a solid experience, it is always very important to meditate every day or at least every other day for at least thirty minutes. Then you will not lose the experience that you have gained and will keep making progress.

If you continue to observe a thirty-minute meditation session every day, you will have an effective meditation that will transform your life and unite you with the blessings of the Buddha of Loving-Kindness. For those whose hearts are open, you will be a continuous source of peace and joy because of your own heart of pure loving-kindness.

Appendix:
The Twelve Stages of Meditation on Loving-Kindness

Use the four meditative powers: images, words, feelings, and belief.

Stage 1. Develop the right attitude, an enlightened attitude, by deciding with conviction to meditate on loving-kindness for the benefit of all beings.

Stage 2. Bring back your mind to your body and fill both with peace and strength.

Stage 3. Visualize the Buddha of Loving-Kindness and his omniscient wisdom, unconditional love, and limitless blessing power as the reflection of the enlightened nature and qualities of your own mind.

Stage 4. Pray with devotion to the Buddha by opening your heart and invoking his blessings.

Stage 5. Receive the blessings of the Buddha by visualizing and believing that you are receiving infinite beams of blessing light of loving-kindness in various colors emitted from the Buddha's body.

Stage 6. Transform your body and mind into a body of blessing light filled with joyful heat energies and the mind of loving-kindness. Your body is pure, clear, translucent, radiant, and intangible.

Stage 7. Enjoy breathing the waves of the powerful blessing energies—the waves of loving-kindness—and transform the energies of stages five and six into an active energy force that purifies, heals, and awakens your body and mind.

Stage 8. Enjoy the sounds of the vibration of the blessing-energy waves, the waves of loving-kindness.

Stage 9. Offer loving-kindness to a loved one by sharing the Buddha's blessing light and energies with unconditional love.

Stage 10. Offer loving-kindness to others and to all by sharing the Buddha's blessing light and energy, and then transform everything into the Blissful Pure Land.

Stage 11. Contemplate by simply resting in the awareness of the feeling of peace or openness, the result of the meditation, without grasping at it or thinking about it.

Stage 12. Dedicate the merit to others and make aspirations.

List of Audio Tracks

The downloadable audio program includes essential Buddhist teachings on loving-kindness along with four meditation tools and a guided loving-kindness meditation in twelve stages. You can download the tracks at www.shambhala.com/healingpower.

1. Shambhala Publications Presents (0:31)
2. Loving-Kindness Is Wishing Joy for All (10:39)
3. Avalokiteshvara: A Symbol of Universal Love (3:44)
4. The Benefits of Loving-Kindness (15:24)
5. Everything Is an Embodiment of Loving-Kindness (5:59)
6. Our Conceptual Mind and Our Enlightened Mind (10:52)
7. Four Tools of Meditation: Positive Images, Words, Feelings, and Trust (10:02)
8. Preliminary Instructions (5:31)
9. Developing the Right Attitude (1:44)
10. Bringing the Mind Back to the Body (6:30)

Notes

In these notes, the titles of works cited are indicated by abbreviations, the key to which can be found in the References. For instance, "YD" stands for *Yon tan rin po ch'e'i mdzod dga' ba'i ch'ar*.

When paginations from traditional Tibetan are cited, the abbreviated title is followed by the folio number. Where relevant, the front or back of the folio is indicated by *a* or *b*, respectively; and then the line number follows the slash mark. An example is DPK 168b/6.

Preface

1. DP pp 1/19.
2. KG ff. 22a/3.

1. An Introduction to Loving-Kindness

1. YD pp. 38/17.
2. According to TZG ff. 19b.6 and ff. 20b/4 and GC pp.294/9, there are three kinds of loving-kindness: (1) The thought of loving-kindness for all beings, as a mother toward her child, is called the "loving-kindness of thinking of the beings." (2) Meditators who have achieved high spiritual attainment—from the first through the seventh *bhumi*—realize all as unreal, but with loving-kindness they serve

beings to realize the true nature. That is called "loving-kindness of thinking of the Dharma [true nature]." (3) Masters whose realizations have reached the eighth and beyond the eighth *bhumi* will have no concepts but will fulfill the needs of others through the power of spontaneously present compassion because of their past aspirations, as a wish-fulfilling jewel fulfills the needs of people without concepts. That is called "the loving-kindness with no concept."

3. DPK ff. 168b/6.

4. TRG pp. 106/2.

5. SB pp. 53/12.

2. The Twelve Stages of Guided Meditation on Loving-Kindness

1. DP pp. 1/19.

2. The image of the Buddha of Loving-Kindness is not limited to one form. There are images and visualizations of the Buddha in different forms, such as in peaceful and wrathful forms; male and female forms; with one head or eleven heads; with two arms, four arms, or a thousand arms; standing and sitting; and in various colors. But here we are using the most popular form from the Tibetan tradition.

3. TR pp. 331a/4: "Visualize [the Buddha], as though he appears, but with no reality." TR 330/5: "The palace is clear, like rainbow light, in the sphere of emptiness. There is no outside or inside, as it is translucent." TR 339/1: "The palace is made of five wisdom lights that appear [but not solid], like illusion, reflection, water-moon, and rainbow."

4. PZ ff. 147b/6: "O men and women of good families—if you recite, remember, or think of this mantra [or six-syllable prayer] even for one time in your mind, if you write it and

keep it on your body or if you pay respect to it—with devotion—then the ill effects of the five heinous deeds and all the secondary [negative] deeds will be purified. You will not take rebirth in any place of suffering such as the three inferior realms or [life with] eight kinds of bondages. You will be free from dangers from human beings, beasts, nonhuman beings, sickness, and negative spirits."

5. TG pp. 354/16.

6. OK ff. 196b/1.

7. BY pp. 58/12.

8. Quoted *"gSer phreng-tantra"* in TRD ff. 46b/3: "Due to grasping at the 'self' of blue, white, yellow, red, and green lights, they have spontaneously appeared as the five gross elements—namely, space, water, earth, fire, and air."

9. LC pp. 306/4.

10. TG 356/6 and TG 356/12.

11. In PZ ff. 148a/1, the Buddha said, "If you recite OM MANI PADME HUNG, you will behold Avalokiteshvara. At the time of your death you will take rebirth in the Blissful Pure Land. Do not entertain doubts, hesitations, or reservations about this."

12. BP 6b/3.

13. MRN pp. 190/10.

14. TG 357/5, TG 358/16, and TG 360/17.

15. RZ ff. 243b/3: "The actual Avalokiteshvara and the source of his manifestations is present at the side of Amitabha Buddha [in the Blissful Pure Land]."

16. KJ pp. 376/18 and pp. 89/10.

References

BP   *Byang ch'ub sems dpa'i spyod pa la 'jug pa* by Shantideva. Tibet: Woodblock print of Dodrupchen Monastery.

BY   "Bla rnam la nye bar mkho ba'i yi ge," by Jigme Tenpe Nyima (third Dodrupchen), in *rDo grub ch'en gsung 'bum*, vol. 4. China: Sitron Mirig Publishing, Chendu, 2003.

DP   *Dharmapada*, translated by Chhimed Rigdzin Lama. India: Center Institute of Higher Tibetan Studies, 1982.

DPK   Dam pa'i ch'os padma dkar po. mDo sDe section, vol. Ja. Kanjur Collection (Dege edition).

GC   *Yon tan mdzod 'grel rgya mtsho'i ch'u thig*. China: Sitron Mirig Publishing, Chendu, 1999.

KG   Kye rdo rje zhes bya ba rgyud kyi rgyal po (Skt. Haivajra). vol. Nga, rGyud Section, Kajur Collection (Dege Edition).

KJ   *mKhas pa'i tshul la 'jug pa'i sgo*, by Mipham Jamyang Namgyal. China: Sitron Mirig Publishing, Chendu, 1989.

LC   *Lam rim ch'en mo*, by Je Tsongkhapa. Taiwan: The Corporate Body of the Buddha Educational Foundation, Taipei, 2000.

MRN   *Mi la res pa'i rNam thar*, by Naljor Rupe Gyenchen. (Tibet: Publisher Unknown).

OK   *Od zer kun tu bkye ba bstan pa.* Vol. Kha. dKon brtsegs, Kajur Collection (Dege Edition).

PD   "dPal seng gi ngor gdams pa," by Jigme Tenpe Nyima. In *rDo grub ch'en gsung 'bum,* vol. 2. China: Sitron Mirig Publishing, Chendu, 2003.

PZ   *Phags pa spyan ras gzigs kyi gzungs,* vol. Tsa, rGyud 'bum section of the Kajur Collection (Dege Edition).

RZ   *Ri ch'os mtshams kyi zhal gdams,* by Raga-asya. India: Trashi Jong Edition.

SB   *gSung 'bum* by Jigme Tenpe Nyima, vol. 2. China: Sitron Mirig Publishing, Chendu, 2003.

TG   "Thog mtha' bar gsum du dGe ba'i gtam," by Paltrul Rinpoche). In *dPal sprul snyan rtsom gches bsdus.* China: Sitron Mirig Publishing, Chendu, 1992.

TR   "Tshor ba rang grol," from the cycle of *dGongs pa rang grol* discovered by Karma Lingpa, vol. Om. India: Sherab Lama.

TRD   *Tshig don rin po che'i mdzod,* by Longchen Rabjam. India: Dodrupchen Edition, Sikkim.

TRG   *Thar pa rin po ch'ei rgyan,* by Sodnam Rinchen (Gampopa). China: Sitron Mirig Publishing, Chendu, 1989.

TZG   *Tshad med bzhi'i rgya ch'er 'grel ba,* vol. Ki, dBu ma section, Tenjur Collection, Dege edition.

YD   *Yon tan rin po ch'e'i mdzod dga' ba'i ch'ar,* by Jigme Lingpa. China: Sitron Mirig Publishing, Chendu, 1999.